KT-074-982

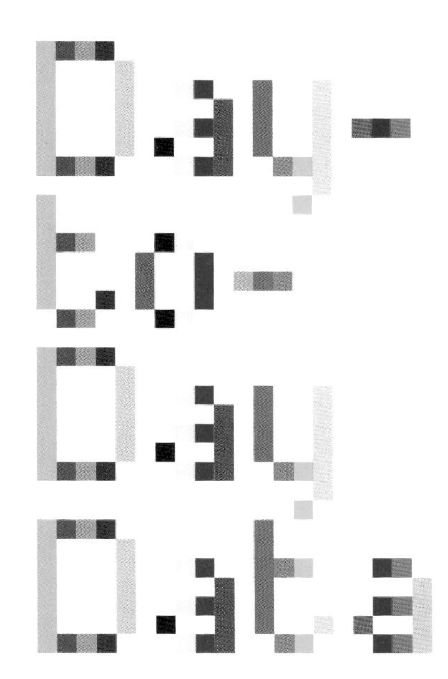

Day-to-Day Data

Abigail Reynolds
Adele Prince
Anders Bojen & Kristoffer Ørum
Christian Nold
Cleo Broda
Ellie Harrison
Gabrielle Sharp

Helen Frosi
Hywel Davies
James Coupe, Hedley Roberts & Rob Saunders
Jem Finer
Kevin Carter
Lucy Kimbell
[illegible]
Richard Dedomenici
Sam Curtis
Therese Stowell
Tim Taylor
Tony Kemplen

Exhibition / Publication / Website

An exhibition of artists who collect, list, database and absurdly analyse the data of everyday life.

Curated by Ellie Harrison

www.daytodaydata.com

Look out for *Eating pizza while watching the news* by Tony Kemplen, which runs throughout this publication.

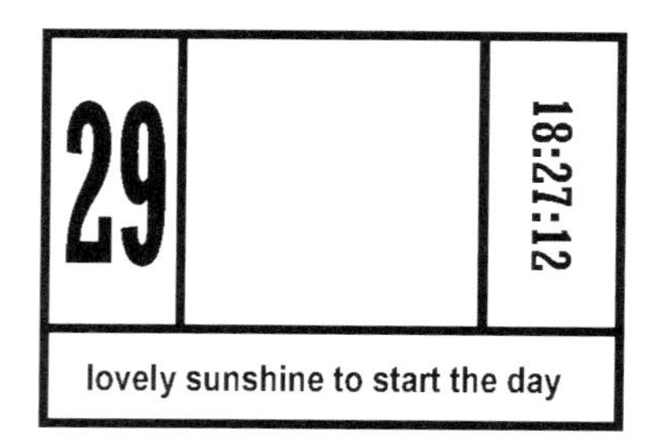

Foreword

Angel Row Gallery is pleased to be working with artist and curator Ellie Harrison to realise the ambitious project that is *Day-to-Day Data*. We are also delighted to be collaborating on the project with Aspex Gallery, Portsmouth, Danielle Arnaud contemporary art, London, SCAN and e-2.

Day-to-Day Data provides a platform for twenty three artists to create new work in three different domains and take part in the project at a number of different levels. The physical exhibition evolves as it moves between the three different gallery spaces. Several artists' projects will be remade to reflect the locality of the three cities visited, and additional artists will join the exhibition at different stages of the tour. The show also extends beyond the gallery onto the internet with four newly commissioned web-based projects and onto the pages of this publication with five new page-based works.

This publication acts as the central point of the whole *Day-to-Day Data* project – a place where all twenty three artists are drawn together and coexist side-by-side. Two specially commissioned essays by Ben Highmore and Kris Cohen help set the scene for the exploration of the artists' ideas and interpretations of *Day-to-Day Data*.

For Angel Row Gallery it was the ambition and breadth of the project that attracted us to work with Ellie Harrison, providing us with the opportunity to continue supporting exciting and challenging contemporary art and also enabling Ellie to develop her individual curatorial practice.

The process of bringing this vast project together reflects her own artistic work in its meticulous planning and organisation – from inviting artists to submit proposals and take part in workshops to explore and develop their own ideas for the project, through to the final selection and commissioning of artists and preparatory work for this publication. Concurrently the website was established and developed to become an integral part of the project and one which will continue to engage with the debates started in the exhibition and publication. It is this considered and methodical approach which underpins the ethos of *Day-to-Day Data*, and which can be traced throughout the works of all the artists and essayists.

For Aspex and indeed for every gallery, the collection of visitor figures, audience analysis and market research are daily activities. *Day-to-Day Data* demonstrates to us a world obsessed with information. Involvement with this project enables Aspex to make a direct connection between the activities undertaken in our office and that which takes place in our gallery. It is no coincidence that the new office mantra is 'we must all learn to love DATA'.

Danielle Arnaud contemporary art is located in the unusual and demanding setting of a central London Georgian house. This fact has meant I have always been apprehensive when artists propose elements of domesticity and everyday life for the gallery. However, after remembering the continuous exercise of list-making when running the gallery and the schizophrenic sense of time this activity engenders, I felt a strong urge to let the artists in *Day-to-Day Data* invade the intimate spaces of the house with their obsession, absurdity and humour. Furthermore, two of the artists, Cleo Broda and Richard Dedomenici, are developing specially commissioned works for the space, including a project linking the gallery to the Durning Library, recently saved from closure by the local community.

After considering the ideas of: day-to-day data alongside public data, intimate moments and personal objects being thrown into the public realm and the private and the public dichotomy of the gallery space itself, it made perfect sense to share the experience of this adventurous touring exhibition.

SCAN is a network of organisations in the South of England delivering projects and initiatives that involve emergent practices and technologies. For us *Day-to-Day Data* provides a very appropriate context to exhibit work from our *9PIN* project. The project, initiated in 2003, is a series of research and development commissions inviting artists to map and connect the organisations and locations in the SCAN network, through the collection of data such as: ambient sounds, sound scenarios, temperature, movement, humidity and data traffic. The work not only reflects the organisations in the network, but also demonstrates a contemporary interest in the way in which data can be manipulated and interpreted through visuals and sound.

We would again like to thank Ellie Harrison, the artists and essayists for their continued commitment to the *Day-to-Day Data* project, and e-2 and the Arts Council England National Touring Programme for their support.

Jim Waters and Helen Jones, Angel Row Gallery
Jo Bushnell, Aspex Gallery
Danielle Arnaud
Helen Sloan, SCAN

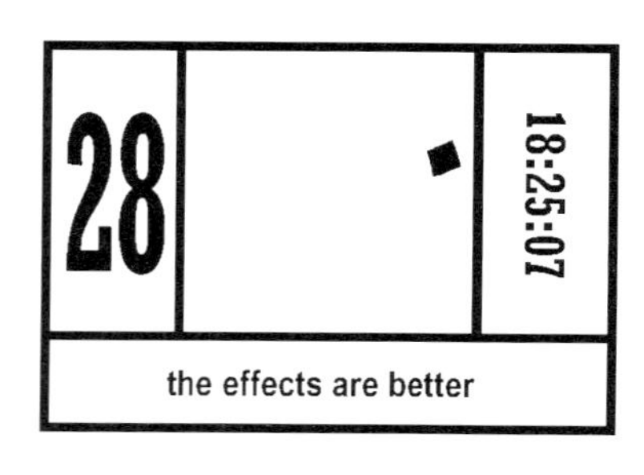

Curator's Introduction

The idea for *Day-to-Day Data* began to emerge towards the end of my postgraduate study at Goldsmiths College in 2003. I had developed an interest, within my own practice, in the documentation and analysis of small or insignificant events from within my own daily routine, creating and manipulating what I termed the 'data of everyday life'.

I was reaching the end of a year-long durational project called *The Daily Quantification Records*; where each day I collected data about my daily habits and bodily state. I was interested in the way the experience of A DAY could be quantified and abstractly represented through the information displayed. p. 32

I consider the idea of *Day-to-Day Data* as two parts which can be broken down and analysed separately: the day-to-day and the data, the subject matter and the methodology. This publication aims to explore the contrasts and crossovers between what the artists have chosen to study and the way in which they have chosen to study it. And how, through the application of a scientific or methodical approach to objects, events or experiences which a normal scientist (or normal person, for that matter) may well overlook, can lead to an absurd or humorous new vision of the everyday life we are all accustomed to.

For this publication, all of the *Day-to-Day Data* artists have been asked to write about their projects in terms of these two distinct areas. Considering first what has drawn them to the subject matter of their investigation and then revealing their own data collection and analysis methodology.

A thorough exploration of the two areas of the *Day-to-Day Data* theme is provided through two specially commissioned essays: Ben Highmore, the authority on everyday life theory, looks at the varied subject matter of *Day-to-Day Data* in his essay *Unprocessed Data: Everyday Life in the Singular*. Kris Cohen, sociologist and researcher into the ritual of photo-blogging on the web, addresses the question of why artists have chosen to create and work with data in his essay *Better the Data you Know...*

Ellie Harrison

Unprocessed Data: Everyday Life in the Singular

Ben Highmore

Day-to-Day

The everyday has been there all the time; it is the world hidden in plain view. If, at the moment, it is becoming the focus of a certain amount of attention (from artists and academics, for instance) then we should remember that this is nothing new, and that artists (think of Picasso's use of newspaper and wallpaper) and social investigators (think of those massive Victorian studies of the habits and habitats of the working class) have been scrutinising the everyday for years. And yet the everyday (yours, mine, and theirs) often exists in the shadows, relatively free from our own scrutiny. Everyday life tends towards the unnoticed; its way of being seems to crave our daily inattention, and its natural environment is most often the unexamined life. And when it is scrutinised it is inevitably transformed. The half-awake and half-ignored daily ablutions become something different when their traces are measured with precision, for instance, in the work of Mary Yacoob (*Trace Elements*). And the spots and markings on a banana take on a different patina when scrutinised as runic signs or maps for divination in the work of p. 44 Helen Frosi (*Life / Lotto*).

Ordinarily, as unexamined life, you could say that everyday life harbours the vast range of attitudes that make up 'normal life', while also working to maintain *ideas* of what constitutes normal life (ideas which, of course, may have little to do with actuality). Everyday life is both ordinary and extraordinary. Indeed, properly speaking, it is the place where the extraordinary becomes ordinary (who, for instance, doesn't have an everyday life?) and where the ordinary is finally ready to be recognised as extraordinary. While it presents itself as the great swath of the unexceptional, everyday life needs only a little jiggling for it to reveal most of us as exceptions, or, more routinely, as contradictions: the arch rationalist who will talk of illness, disaster and death and quickly search out for a piece of wood to touch (increasingly difficult in certain environments); the obsessive tidier whose bathroom is filthy. Everyday life is the realm of loosely held together contradictions and the realm of low-resolution ideology, usually paraded as 'common sense' and 'nature'. And this is more or less the problem of the everyday: endless peculiarity meets the endless 'quiet' reproduction of social norms. Which is it then? Is the everyday to be mined for its mass of minor infractions of social norms, its ceaseless generation of idiosyncrasies? Or should we recognise that in the everyday lurk the most trenchant ideological beliefs, the most hard-to-fight bigotries? Isn't there something insidious and surreptitious, as well as ferociously depressing, about the way racism and sexism have kept a stronghold in the everyday long after substantial victories had been won at the level of legislation? Any attempt to celebrate indiscriminately the

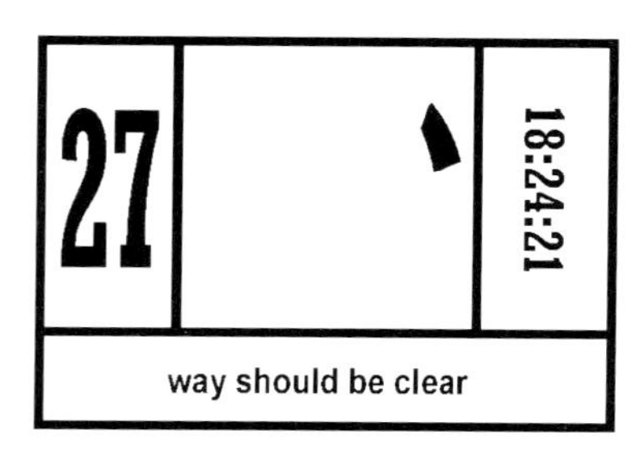

everyday needs to face the fact that it also provides a safe-house for our very worst attitudes and activities.

Contradiction, then, might be seen to be at the very heart of everyday life, and it is fitting that the artists of *Day-to-Day Data* are adept at exploiting the power of the unresolved (and irresolvable) contrast. p. 72 Tea, as used by Tim Taylor (*Our Daily Drugs (Morning Action Patinas)*), produces subtle visual haikus on a daily basis: it is also a product that bears the history of Western imperialism and the continued uneven relationship between the West and Asia. Soap p. 24 powder, as seen by Anders Bojen & Kristoffer Ørum (*Detergent (Real imaginary system)*), contains a whole cosmology of strange biomorphic forms, unsettling satellites, a Ferris wheel and various bubbled figures, and yet it remains a commodity, available in any supermarket around the world. Soap was an instrumental ingredient in the everyday cultural colonisation of India and Africa, for instance: it carries its history as a secret cargo.[1] Soap powder is the example that Henri Lefebvre, author of various volumes of the critique of everyday life, often gave for the way that the commodity is 'thoroughly penetrating the details of daily life'. Soap, tea, and sugar,[2] with their colonial histories and neo-colonial presents, are evidence of the way that imperialism and capitalism colonise the recesses of the everyday through the most ordinary materials. And yet, these ordinary materials and their possibilities are not, in the end, simply reducible to forces of imperial capitalism and its derivatives.

When day-to-day objects became commodities they were encouraged to dream (so as to obscure the shabby and exploitative conditions of their production), but this dreamworld quickly surpassed the pragmatic need for subterfuge. The world of things has conjured a fantasy world of elaborate dimensions. Soap powders can contain Ferris wheels, just as a new car can make you more attractive. There is an excess of dreams out there. And the ability of objects to dream has not just served a world determined by profit; it has given expressive potential to the world of things. Thus when Cleo Broda (*Personal Soft Data Archive System*) charts her emotional attachment to the things she is letting go of, she also recognises their attachment to her. And when Adele Prince (*Trolley Spotting*) maps p. 22 the routes of deserter shopping trolleys as they head for the countryside, waylaid in the shallow streams on the edge of town or caught in back alleys, she recognises the trolley's dream to escape the army discipline of the supermarket. Gabrielle Sharp's (*Losing it* p. 36 *in London*) investigation of mislaid and misplaced objects uncovers a treasure trove of mnemonic objects silently waiting for their mediums and mediators who will once again let them speak. It is this unpredictable and in some ways unmanageable remainder that is one of the subjects of *Day-to-Day Data*.

Data-Day

Everyday life seems to have a peculiar penchant for data; just as data seems always ready to be seduced by the daily. Trawling through the mass of facts that circulate on the internet, the most readily available seem to consist of the mass-regularities of the daily. For instance it turns out that US

1. See Anne McClintock, *Imperial Leather: Race, Gender and Sexuality in the Colonial Contest* (London and New York: Routledge, 1995).
2. Henri Lefebvre gives the example of someone buying sugar for demonstrating the way that a seemingly banal moment of daily life is connected to both global capitalism and personal desire and memory (and everything else in between) – Henri Lefebvre, *Critique of Everyday Life: Volume 1*, translated by John Moore (London: Verso, 1991), p. 57. This passage was originally published in French in the 1958 second edition of the book.

citizens drink 35 billion cups of tea each year and use 68 million kilograms of tea to do this. More interesting might be the 'fact' that over 1,000 tonnes of space dust falls to earth each year and that this might be responsible for flu epidemics (I imagine that a few tonnes must be falling into the cups of tea). Alternatively you might be fascinated to know that dogs living in the UK produce 1,000 tonnes of faeces every day (collectively, that is). Data, as used to map regularities, quantities, frequencies, probabilities, and so on, produces a landscape rich in surreal potential. It also maps a landscape that is useful to social planners, the stock market, trans-national retailers, security services, practitioners of cultural studies, and so on.

The everyday use of the word 'data' has a quality which is similar to the way that the term 'the everyday' is used. Data, as my dictionary informs me, is a plural noun that is often treated as a singular one. It is therefore grammatically incorrect to claim a single piece of information as data; it is more correctly a datum. Facts about tea drinking and dog excreting are produced via a range of information: they coalesce as a composite form – one giant dog, one giant turd – one monstrous orchestrated chorus of tea drinking. The term 'the everyday' exhibits some of the same qualities: essentially plural (a single day clearly won't do) it often seems to veil itself in the singular – as if one everyday belongs to us all, as if everyday life is not characterised by unevenness and conflict. But, and it is a big but, this is not a plural noun becoming 'singular' by stressing the material particularity of an object existing at a specific moment. It is the singular as an abstract entity that works to veil the concrete singular that we all exist in. And it is against this 'abstract singular' that the artists of *Day-to-Day Data* are most thoroughly engaged as champions of the insistent materiality of the 'concrete singular'.

One way out of the abstractions of data processing (and one step nearer to the concrete everyday) is to reverse its operational logic. This is what Lucy Kimbell does with her *Physical Bar Charts*. She begins with the abstractions of processed data and works to make this material concrete by getting visitors to claim and possess specific bits of datum. Abstraction becomes subtraction and physical data is 'returned' to the source. Another way out of abstraction is to literalise the process of data collection in the way that Borges suggested when he imagined a map being made that was as detailed and of exactly the same scale as the land it represented.[3] This is the tactic of Sam Curtis as he proceeds to conduct his own *IDUK* census by personally counting everyone in the UK. Yet another way is to discover surprising concrete actualities in the abstractions of numerically raw and random data: this is what Richard Dedomenici does when he 'discovers' an uncanny conglomeration of nail salons surrounding the satellite cities on the edge of London (*Nail Salon Belt*) and protecting them from metropolitan encroachment.

p. 66

p. 64

Routine Matter

As defenders of the 'concrete singular' the artists of *Day-to-Day Data* share a number

26

18:23:35

unimpressed with the debate

of similar manoeuvres. In their fight against the abstractions of mainstream data-processing they have all found ways of short-circuiting the absorption of datum into data. Probably the one element that unites all these artists is a vigorous emphasis on materiality – on the stuff-ness of stuff. Hence it is no uncanny coincidence to find that among the various projects here it is often the substances of daily life that are most emphatically stressed (soap powder, tea, toothpaste, bananas, etc.). One of the main effects of abstraction is the production of a human subject that is similarly abstracted – a disembodied, virtual being – and one of the best ways of re-embodying this human subject is to remind ourselves that we all eat, drink, get ill, excrete, digest, sneeze, get hot, smell, wash, secrete, have sex, absorb, process proteins, fats, minerals, vitamins, have babies, bleed, get old, get fit and so on. Emphasising the materiality of bodies is, and this may seem counter intuitive, also a way of defending the everyday against the ideology of individualism and identity (which is another abstraction of the singular). By foregrounding the literal consumptions and productions of the body, the body becomes a site of interconnectivity that throws into question the very premise of identity (which is, according to psychoanalysis, based on fantasy relations that produce an imagined sense of wholeness). p. 26 Christian Nold's *Bio Mapping* device, for instance, measures the body's Galvanic Skin Response – an index of physical excitement – and connects this to specific geographical space. Such bodily responses are not the signs of a consciousness or agency reacting to place; they are the body's 'own' form of dialogue. Our bodies give 'us' away precisely because 'we' do not control them: who is it that can voluntarily blush? In a similar vein, p. 32 Ellie Harrison's *Daily Data Log* is a record of the material conditions of the body – its inputs and outputs – its irruptions – its affective states – as they are measured via a number of low tech instruments, including the artist's subjective view. Affectivity is the body producing meaning (by being embarrassed, by laughing, by being anxious): it is the material unconscious of the everyday – a material source that is undervalued precisely because it doesn't seem to be produced or controlled by the subject of rational thought. The eradication of the irrational and the inefficient (as well as the anti-social) in material day-to-day life is the topic of *Daily Efficiency and Behavioural Analysis, Self-evaluation Checklist (DEBASC)*. It is a checklist of such magnitude, of such competing demands that to embark on it will send you spiralling into the world of pathological inefficiency and anti-social and irrational behaviour.

p. 68 Therese Stowell's *Emotional Stimuli and Responses Over 24-Hour Period* – an attempt to produce a diagrammatic account of her emotional and affective life over an entire day – is portraiture performed by an anthropological ecologist. Pregnancy (which is one aspect of the 'state' of Stowell during the 24 hours) is a condition that makes vivid a more general truth: 'we' (though the unification of this pronoun would need to be undone) are tough and fragile, chemical and ideational, life-supporting and life-supported – we are ourselves a complex ecosystem living within a larger and even more complex ecosystem. Whether or not such ecosystems can become predictable is the

3. 'The Cartographers Guilds struck a Map of the Empire whose size was that of the Empire, and which coincided point for point with it', Jorge Luis Borges, *A Universal History of Infamy* (1935) translated by Andrew Hurley, in *Collected Fictions* (New York: Viking Penguin, 1998), p. 325.

question posed by James Coupe, Hedley Roberts & Rob Saunders as they monitor the everyday activities of office life in various organisations in *9PIN++*. For Stowell the 'individual' is forever spilling outward, producing surprising connections: for Coupe, Roberts & Saunders complex ecologies are treated as organism-like entities that might be habit forming in their routine, day-to-day life.

Agitated Layers of Air

It is tempting to see the term 'material' as pointing to the physical actuality of life – for instance, the pizza in Tony Kemplen's work (*Eating pizza while watching the news*) – and to see the world of images and words – the TV news items in Kemplen's work – as somehow at one remove from the material. Yet by juxtaposing pizza and TV news Kemplen plays on the non-fit between the two (the necessary contingency of their coinciding) while also suggesting that materially we ingest both, both are matter that we absorb. It is worth looking to Marx and Engels for an understanding of materialism that would understand language as a base material of existence: 'From the start the "spirit" is afflicted with the curse of being "burdened" with matter, which here makes its appearance in the form of agitated layers of air, sounds, in short, of language.'[4] 'Agitated layers of air', as a base material of the day-to-day, is the emphasis of the sound artist Hywel Davies (*Basic Set*) as he weaves together what film theorists call 'diegetic sound' (the sound – including 'wild sound' – recorded on location) into orchestrated soundscapes.

p. 48

It is this vital relationship to the practical materiality of sound and language that is also emphasised in Kevin Carter's work (*De do do do, de da da da (They're meaningless and all that's true)*) around the chatter of his pre-verbal 11 month old baby.

p. 54

Language is the material of the day-to-day from the pops and fizzes of baby 'talk' (a musically affective sequence of cadences) to the cosmological language of the stars. Jem Finer (*On Earth as in Heaven*) literally brings the 'stars down to earth'.[5] By tracing celestial bodies onto the earth's surface by dint of shared names (but this time instead of naming astral bodies the names tag cars, streets, people, and so on) he maps new constellations, which though essentially random, are also 'written in the stars'. Finer produces maps that simultaneously reconfigure the cosmic as the banal world of the day-to-day while also revealing the day-to-day world as linguistically saturated by the cosmic (1,000 tonnes of space dust falls to earth each year). These everyday earth-bound names remain heavenly. It is this fascinating and facile linguistic world that Abigail Reynolds pictures when she tabulates the strange permutations connected to the word 'table' (*Dictionary Ranges. Diagram of 'table'*). In this way that slight slippage that seems to occur between 'word' and 'world' points to an actuality: for Reynolds a word is already (very nearly) a world.

p. 52

p. 18

Coda

The artists of *Day-to-Day Data* are crusaders fighting the abstracting impulses of sociological quantifiers and market researchers alike. Like quixotic evangelists they are taking on the powerful forces in our present

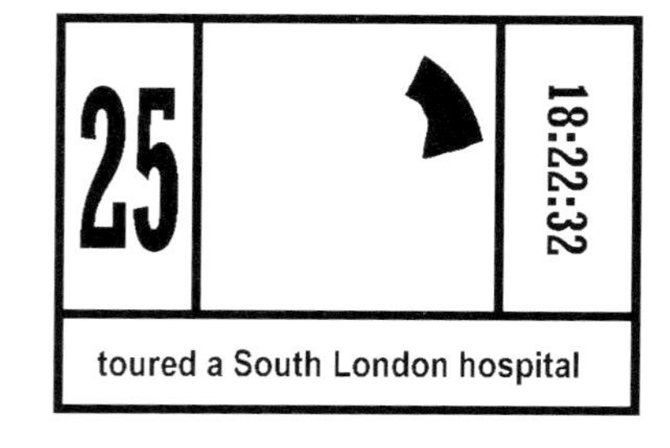

moment that would work to sever everyday life from the bodies that inhabit it, and empty it of its sensuous specificity. If the shopping mall and the security services are interested in bodies as abstract indices that need to be controlled and compelled (in a variety of ways and for a variety of reasons) *Day-to-Day Data* wants bodies that pulse with their own idiosyncratic possibilities and proclivities. These are bodies that interact with a physical and ideational world that is as material as they are.

The artists of *Day-to-Day Data* reveal the everyday world to be made up of concrete singularities. The concrete, here, is a world where bodies are simultaneously biological and cultural, where 'things' are at once dumb-matter and agents that act in the world, and where language is a matter of practice and a practical matter. And the singular is revealed as the very opposite of both the false unity of the abstract singular ('woman', 'the British', 'India', 'youth', and so on) and the monadic fragment of individualism. The concrete singular of the everyday is the singular lattice of connections and disconnections that always exist in specific times and places: it is the everyday as a complex of competing, conflicting, consensual, contrasting and conflicting concretions. It is the living world of material social relations. Who knew that data could be this sensual?

4. Karl Marx and Frederick Engels, *The German Ideology* (London: Lawrence and Wishart, 1970). The text was written in 1845.

5. Coincidentally or not this is the title of a long essay written by Theodor Adorno in 1953 which analyses the astrology column of the *Los Angeles Times* as part of a mass everyday irrationalism. See Theodor W. Adorno, *The Stars Down to Earth and Other Essays on the Irrational in Culture* (London and New York: Routledge, 1994).

Better the Data you Know…

Kris Cohen

Does 'data' strike you as a cold or somehow impoverished title for artworks which, among other things, communicate the pathos of an artist's history of separation anxiety (Cleo Broda, *Personal Soft Data Archive System*), invite laughter at the idea that an undiscovered ring of nail salons around London is the force which protects the suburbs p. 64 from urban sprawl (Richard Dedomenici, *Nail Salon Belt*), or which propose grandly (or the opposite of grandly) to map the heavens upon p. 52 the earth (Jem Finer, *On Earth as in Heaven*)? Isn't this exactly what is eye catching about the title *Day-to-Day Data*: the fire and ice tension between the strange intimacies of day-to-day life and the suggestion that what we should be concerned with here is, in fact, cold, hard data? On the other hand, the idea of a corporation amassing consumer data or a government collecting data on its citizens is so familiar as to seem almost natural. How did *data* get so far away, so impersonal?[1] How did *data* get such a cold inhuman heart, so much in tension with life as it is lived?[2]

And yet, against these de-personalising tendencies in data, the spectacle of individuals collecting and presenting data about themselves is an increasingly common one, especially on the internet. To take three popular examples, consider *blogs*, *flickr* and *audioscrobbler*.[3] For whatever else these sites are or do, they are predicated on the idea that individuals will want to collect data on themselves in the form of diaries, photographs, links, preferences, tastes and relationships and, moreover, will find compelling reasons to do this collecting publicly. All out of proportion to their alleged banality, individuals' efforts in this direction have been the target of disdain, parody, and summary dismissal.[4] Why the resistance?[5] One answer is teleological, about the uses of *data*. The scenario of the individual collecting data compels us to ask, with almost unavoidable suspicion: what does he or she want with all that data, and, more to the point, what can WE-THE-PUBLIC possibly do with the results? In the case of *Day-to-Day Data*, I'm not sure the answer 'well, it's Art' quite gets us off the hook. If the idea of a government or a corporation collecting data is comparatively unremarkable, I think this is because (whatever our opinions about them) institutions come with a kind of inbred telos, an assumed purposiveness. We say: they need data to do business, to generate new product ideas, to provide public services, to defend the nation's borders. But, whatever the answer, these Big Entities (B. E.) seem to evade the teleological question about *data* without the question ever needing to be asked – and it is always a significant accomplishment when potential lines of inquiry are shut down. Not that challenges do not occur, but they are exceptional rather than expected. Corporations and governments appear to have a natural right to *data*.

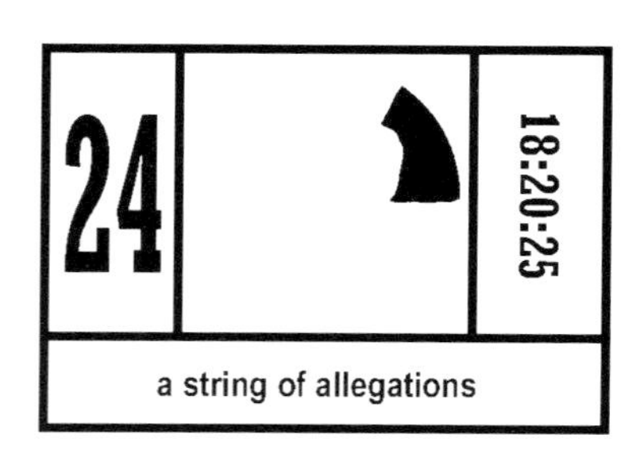

These structural underpinnings of *data* are important – they are, I think, exactly what the artworks in *Day-to-Day Data* ask us to recognise. But there is something else. Corporations and governments, two of the usual suspects of data collection, claim (in several senses and in varying degrees of bad faith) to act on behalf of PUBLIC interests – that is, in the interests of consumers or citizens. Data, then, in its most naturalised locution, appears to be *about* the public, *for* the public or both – although rarely made available to the public.[6] For our purposes, I think Michael Warner provides one of the most useful descriptions of how *data's* publics function: 'Public discourse… is poetic. By this I mean not just that it is self-organizing… but that… all discourse or performance… must characterize the world in which it attempts to circulate and it must attempt to realize that world through address.'[7] When Warner refers to publics as 'poetic world making', he is writing against the common-sense idea that publics simply exist – naturally, socially or by fiat – and that individuals exist passively within them. In Warner's terms, the creation of data about or for the public – census data, market data – is one of the many activities which substantiates that public – which defines us as a national, global, ethnic or consumer body. *Data* is, therefore, an instrument of our passivity in the face of B.E. In describing us, it seems to constitute us.

In contrast to the discourses of B.E., individual or personal modes of speech uncomfortably occupy publics, as evidenced (to take one current example) by the number of people who pillory bloggers for being narcissistic.[8] If the works in *Day-to-Day Data* at first appear peculiar or flippant or even narcissistic, I think it is because they appear to violate the requirement that data be either about or for the public – that is, we tend to believe that public matters exclude the work of individuals. Common uses of the terms 'public' and 'private' serve to enforce the irrelevance of individuals' activities to public life, to erect a prophylactic barrier between the two realms (e.g. 'do whatever you want in the PRIVACY of your own home'). Warner again: 'It is often thought, especially by outsiders,

1. I use italics to indicate that the intended sense of data, here and subsequently, is twofold: both data-the-word (its connotations and denotations) as well as data-the-concept (its history and social uses).

2. In order to proceed from this point, we might seem to need a definition of *data*. But to think about *data* beyond its naturalising connotations, as I believe *Day-to-Day Data* asks us to do, requires not a definition of *data* so much as an armature, a diagram of the networks *data* sits within. Schematically, these would be: 1. the people or things *data* describes, 2. the descriptions or representations themselves (the forms data takes), and 3. the ways those representations are used, their effects and intended effects. We will be more concerned here with the operations of data, its actions – how it is made and what it effects. The works in *Day-to-Day Data* encourage this perspective.

3. Blogs or web logs are frequently updated personal web sites which often take the form of a diary and which have been one of the most popular and hyped internet technologies over the past five years. www.flickr.com is a photo-sharing community. www.audioscrobbler.com is a 'free service that builds up a detailed profile of your musical tastes' and creates networks of affinity between users based on those tastes.

4. Many bloggers and flickr users describe their sites in these terms: as amassings of personal data in the form of photographs, memories, dates, references, histories, etc. At the time of writing, I am nearing the end of two years of research on blogs and bloggers, during which I have been especially interested in the uses of photography, and so latterly have come to study flickr (thanks to the Economic and Social Research Council for my current research fellowship). If I speak about those kinds of sites here, then, it is not only because they have been on my mind, but because I think the questions they have raised with regard to data and the interplay between individuals and publics are highly relevant to, if not co-extensive with, the concerns of *Day-to-Day Data*. For more information on this research, see: www.photosleavehome.blogspot.com; 'What does the photoblog want?' in *Media, Culture & Society*, Winter 2005; and 'A Welcome for Blogs' in Continuum special issue on 'Counter-heroics and Counter-professionalism in Cultural Studies', June 2006.

5. There has also, of course, been massive, sometimes hyperbolic support.

6. This was a central criticism, for instance, in the recent struggle over ID cards in Australia. Simon Davies writes about it here: http://wearcam.org/envirotech/simon_davies_opposition_to_id_card_schemes.htm

7. Michael Warner, *Publics and Counterpublics* (New York: Zone Books, 2000), p. 113-4.

8. Narcissism, as I quote its use here, and as it has been commonly used to criticise blogs, tends not to reference the extensive psychoanalytic literature on narcissism. Popular criticism which invokes narcissism tends, most tellingly, to forget that Narcissus, in the founding myth, didn't realise that his love was self-love. Narcissus' self-regard occurred to him, mistakenly but earnestly, as the loving regard of another. In the argument I am making about individuals in relation to data and publics, this ambiguity between the individual's regard for self and his or her regard for others is significant. Narcissism, as a concept, contains this ambiguity and is therefore a far more telling epithet than its wielders realise. People who call blogs narcissistic deploy a comparatively one-way definition which connotes an unhealthy interest in oneself and an unseemly display of this self-interest in public. Here is one example from a newspaper article: http://flacklife.blogspot.com/2005/02/ottawa-citizen-gets-it-utterly-wrong.html. The article quotes Sam Vaknin, author of *Malignant Self Love: Narcissism Revisited*. Even though his book's title pretty much says it all, here is what Vaknin says about the internet: 'The Internet allows us to replicate ourselves and our words… to communicate instantly with thousands… and, in general, to realize some of our narcissistic dreams and tendencies'. The author of the article later elaborates Vaknin's idea: 'Similarly, weblogs (or blogs) allow individuals to indulge grandiose fantasies of who they are, cataloguing the nuances of their lives – real or imagined – for all to see'.

that the public display of private matters is a debased narcissism, a collapse of decorum, expressivity gone amok, the erosion of any distinction between public and private'.[9]

One artist commonly accused of narcissism is Cindy Sherman, who infamously stars in all of her *Untitled Film Stills* and in most of the rest of her work.[10] If the artworks in *Day-to-Day Data* appear to similarly disdain publics - appear, that is, narcissistic - do they reference the artist in the same ways that Sherman's work references the artist?

Leo Steinberg suggests that we understand a public's difficulty with new and unfamiliar works of art as a 'sense of loss, of sudden exile' from what that public knows or believes.[11] In this light, complaints about art's narcissism are instructive. They allow us to ask: what has been lost, from what familiar or comfortable notions have we been exiled? In the perhaps discomfiting proposition that data might be thought of as art, or visa versa, I think two things have been lost, or must be given up: the belief that data is neutral or un-invested by power and the belief that affairs of public life should exist apart from the subjective taint of individuals' private affairs ('why should we-the-public p. 32 want to know what Ellie Harrison did today; why should we want to know what any blogger did today; what does it have to do with us?').[12] In opposition, *Day-to-Day Data* suggests 1. that data is always made, and that the making inevitably has vested interests; and 2. that publics rely on the day-to-day lives of individuals far more than they have been willing to recognise.

Now I think we are in a position to appreciate what I take to be one of *Day-to-Day Data's* central assertions. We can think of it this way, answering a previous question: the artworks in *Day-to-Day Data* do indeed reference the artist as Sherman's *Untitled Film Stills* reference the artist: not simply as artist, nor narcissistic subject, nor content (as critics would have it), but as the vector along which viewers are invited to think about themselves as connected to the larger systems which seem to subsume them. In Sherman's work, these include visuality, gender, sexuality, Art, film. In *Day-to-Day Data*, the systems addressed are varied, the works alike less in their concern with particular systems than in the way they invert the expected relationship between individual and structure in those systems. That is, they show how structures which appear to encompass individuals, to bestow meaning on us, are actually constituted by individuals, by our actions.[13] This is why the artists in *Day-to-Day Data* present data not as it is, but as it is made - in all cases, they make their own *data*.[14] In this, they exhume the steps by which any form of data becomes, in succession: thinkable, legible, familiar, invisible, and finally, authoritative. Their interest in the day-to-day says that this is how all data is made: step by banal step, in people's day-to-day lives - whether we make it ourselves, or whether we tacitly authorise others to collect it for us. Although, as our experiences with *Day-to-Day Data* will suggest, there is a big difference between doing it ourselves and having data collected for us.

23

18:20:08

leaving Neverland this morning

In this light, *Day-to-Day Data* seems a very serious affair. In which case, whence the show's humour? presents what she calls her *Daily Efficiency and Behavioural Analysis, Self-evaluation Checklist (DEBASC)*, an obviously parodic data entry form. p. 44 Helen Frosi (*Life / Lotto*) tries to divine the winning Lottery numbers from ciphers she finds hidden in the minutiae of her everyday routine. p. 22 Adele Prince (*Trolley Spotting*) literally tracks and maps purloined shopping trolleys. p. 24 Anders Bojen & Kristoffer Ørum (*Detergent (Real imaginary system)*) give the genealogy of a box of detergent. Are they serious, these artists? Better perhaps to ask: what exactly are they serious about? At what is their humour directed?

If their work provokes laughter, it is a kind of laughter frequently heard today. Are blogs serious? Is a flickr group devoted to photographs of food or feet serious?[15] They are, in any case, the subject of serious public discussion: e.g. the transformation of democracy, journalism, property, copyright, creativity, celebrity.[16] If we laugh at the idea that blogs could transform anything, let alone those unwieldy systems, maybe our laughter betrays the limits of our ability or willingness to think about the individual's capacity to act in or on public life – to influence the systems which seem, on the contrary, to encompass and define us.[17]

The artworks in *Day-to-Day Data* stage a vexing irruption of the individual – the artist or viewer, their choices and behaviours – into publics which seem designed specifically to overwrite that very figure. But art discourse has always had some use or other for the personal life of the artist. How then does the individual uniquely inhabit the works of *Day-to-Day Data*? Diversely is one good answer.

p. 26 When Christian Nold invites people to collect data about their own Galvanic Skin Response (a simple measure of stress or excitement), certainly there are different tactics at work than when Ellie Harrison uses daily self-observations to instruct gallery staff to create a live visual display for that day. So, we notice that some of the artists use their own lives as the data source while others look outward.

But *Day-to-Day Data* asks us to think about all of its artists as data collectors, whoever or whatever they collect data about. In the past century, artists have frequently traded the figure of the Artist for a wide array of substitutes.[18] How, then, does the ARTIST-AS-DATA-COLLECTOR guide our reading of these works? Data collection is an additive process; data becomes significant when individual data points melt into the satisfying uniformity of the informational Whole. But in requiring that we learn something about, if not come to care about, the individual lives out of which data is generated, the works in *Day-to-Day Data* counter-intuitively and beautifully resolve an image of the individual out of the uniform

9. Warner, p. 62, op. cit.

10. As Joan Copjec points out in Imagine *There's No Woman: Ethics and Sublimation* (Cambridge, MA: MIT Press, 2002), p. 74.

11. Leo Steinberg, 'Contemporary Art and the Plight of its Public' in *Other Criteria: Confrontations with Twentieth Century Art* (London: Oxford University Press, 1972), p. 7.

12. If these don't seem like losses to you – if they seem like well-learned lessons of a century of anti-Enlightenment thinking – I submit that it is far easier to accept them theoretically than to accept them in one's day-to-day life.

13. Here, I am drawing in part on Bruno Latour's talk 'A Possible Alternative to Social Explanations?' presented at the Centre Launch Party, March 18, 2004, Centre for the Study of Invention and Social Process (CSISP), at Goldsmiths University. Latour criticised the ways people use Big structures – Society, Culture, Art etc. – to explain the behaviours of individuals. He emphasised that those structures which seem to be explanatory are, in fact, what need to be explained.

14. In contrast, for instance, with works of 'data-mining' which focus less on the making of data than on the appropriation and uses of it. For more on data-mining, see: http://en.wikipedia.org/wiki/Datamining

15. For one of many flickr food groups, see: 'What's in your fridge?' at www.flickr.com/groups/88412962@N00; For the foot group, see: www.flickr.com/groups/foot

16. For lots more information on blogs and democracy try googling 'blogs democracy', for blogs and journalism, try 'blogs journalism'; for property and ownership, see any of the writings of Lawrence Lessig at www.lessig.org

17. Whatever is said about the irrelevance or narcissism of blogs, no one seems to have been able to ignore them. *Day-to-Day Data* provides many answers to the question of why blogs vex us so.

18. e.g. the humble manual labourer, the pop celebrity, the scientist, the rock star, the collector (of junk or found objects) etc.

static of *data*. They focus our attention on an inverted picture of process.

Nold's, Kimbell's, Curtis' and Coupe, Roberts & Saunders' works literally cannot be thought apart from considerations of process. In this, they recall Robert Morris' 'The Box with the Sound of its Own Making' (1961). But whereas Morris' box forces us to consider process retroactively, thinking backwards from the conventional art object to the process by which it was made, these four works force us to consider process as the artwork (rather than the unmaking or unmasking of the artwork). Process exists in the experiential p. 26 present of their work: Nold's exists when people take a walk wearing the *Bio Mapping device*; exists when people answer a question by removing a sweet from the *Physical* p. 66 *Bar Charts*; Curtis' exists when people are counted by Curtis himself as part of his *IDUK* census; Coupe, Roberts & Saunders' exists when their *9PIN++* network of computers records or informs the activities of the SCAN network.[19] Each work generates a product (documentation and analysis) but the conventional relationship between process and product has been reversed – the works exist most forcefully in moments of action which involve us as more than onlookers. We could say they are performative if we do not think of the artist as the performer.

By comparison, the other pieces in *Day-to-Day Data* seem to keep process at arm's length, although never out of reach: the documentation or translation of their research guides our reading of the work. All of the works in *Day-to-Day Data*, however, go beyond the old idea of process as a theme internal to art (painting, for instance, has always been about the act of painting). By appropriating processes of data collection which live in other social registers – politics, commerce, science – the works assembled here discuss not just the processes by which an artwork is made, but the processes through which any data is transformed into products, e.g. census charts, segmentation models, new products, gerrymandered voting districts, tighter immigration laws, and so on. In this, *Day-to-Day Data* reveals data's political investments. But more far-reaching still, the works in *Day-to-Day Data* model, exaggerate and thereby lay bare the processes by which we, as individuals, come into relation with the worlds, the B.E. which appear to define us... including the art world. This is what *data* normally accomplishes, be it census data, public opinion polls or market research: by informing us about ourselves, it subsumes us within social registers which appear bigger than individuals, which seem untouchable and unchangeable. To invert this process, I believe, is the broadest ambition of the exhibition's appropriation of *data*. And it is in support of this ambition that *Day-to-Day Data* prioritises the right to create data in the first instance – because whoever makes data makes the publics that data purports merely to describe.

But the first thing we might have noticed about the works in *Day-to-Day Data*, and which I have left until the end, is how they seem to be extreme in one way or another: e.g. ridiculously thorough, exaggeratedly scientific, painfully introspective. To notice this quality of the works is to notice their humour,

which I mentioned before. I think, however, that we can notice this quality differently now: namely, as part of a challenge to the presumptive place of individuals in public life. If they seem absurd, why is this – what would we have to give up to take them seriously? p. 36 If Gabrielle Sharp's hand drawn studies (*Losing it in London*) seem somehow insanely mismatched to the task of tracking and ordering Transport for London's massive collection of lost items, what is the sanity, the proper data, that they swerve from? If Tony Kemplen's documentation of *Eating pizza while watching the news* seems random, then what more sensible data do we imagine he is withholding from us? If, in a very different p. 54 register, Kevin Carter's database of sounds made by his 11 month old son Jake (*De do do do, de da da da (They're meaningless and all that's true)*) seems too personal or too invasive, how do we draw the line between 'relevant' and 'narcissistic', public and private, and in the service of what comfortable distinctions do we draw it where we do?

The pieces in *Day-to-Day Data*, in common with many new forms of personal data collection, are engaged in a type of activity which is forcing a new and lively public reckoning: namely, a reckoning with individuals' attempts – in text, in photographs, in video and mobile and audio blogs, online and off – to create measures of their own worlds, and not just for themselves or their families, but for others to see and use.[20] When Lawrence Lessig defends cultural 'remixing' against new laws which threaten those activities, or when McKenzie Wark gives his manifesto for 'hacking', or when proponents of sousveillance encourage individuals to collect their own data (sousveillance is 'watchful vigilance from underneath'), I hear each championing the kinds of activities which concern the artists in *Day-to-Day Data*: that is, efforts on the part of individuals to record their own observations, to make and measure and analyse culture, society and other B. E. – and to do so (and this, I think, is the critical move) publicly, for others to use.[21] If we resist the idea of artists generating data, or the kinds of data we find in *Day-to-Day Data* – if we are tempted to call them narcissistic or obsessive or glib – I think this resistance says as much about how we esteem individuals as about how we esteem art or artists.

Eve Sedgwick expresses what is at stake in our capacity to recognise individual acts of 'remixing' or 'hacking' or 'sousveillance' or 'day-to-day data collecting': 'What we can best learn from such practices are, perhaps, the many ways selves and communities succeed in extracting sustenance from the objects of a culture – even of a culture whose avowed desire has often been not to sustain them'.[22] The works in *Day-to-Day Data* give us the figure of the data collector, and in the humility of this figure – the absurdity, the banality, the intimacy – we get something much greater: we get the individual artist or viewer or blogger or anyone as a maker of the publics that he or she inhabits. It is a big idea resident in the smallest and unlikeliest of sources; a transformation of the very idea that 'individuals can make a difference'. But this, behind the innocence of its laughter, is what *Day-to-Day Data* can do.

19. SCAN (Southern Collaborative Arts Network). A consortium of arts venues / organisations in southern England www.scansite.org

20. Compare this public airing of personal data to, say, photo albums, which are typically only seen by family and friends.

21. Lawrence Lessig, *Free Culture: How Big Media Uses Technology and the Law to Lock Down Culture and Control Creativity* (New York: The Penguin Press, 2004), available at: www.lessig.org. McKenzie Wark, A Hacker Manifesto (Cambridge, MA: Harvard University Press, 2004). For more information on sousveillance, see Steve Mann writing here: www.chairetmetal.com/cm06/mann-complet.htm. For a less polemical introduction to sousveillance, see: http://en.wikipedia.org/wiki/Sousveillance

22. Eve Sedgwick, 'Paranoid Reading, Reparative Reading' in *Touching Feeling: Affect, Pedagogy, Performativity* (Durham, N.C. and London: Duke University Press, 2003), p. 151-2.

Abigail Reynolds

Born: 1970
Nationality: British
Lives: London
Title: *Dictionary Ranges. Diagram of 'table'*
Location: Installation at all gallery venues
Website: www.abigailreynolds.com

The Oxford English Dictionary (OED) is generally perceived as a fixed authority, but in actuality it is a research project that moves through the shifting terrain of written language. The specific task of the OED is to track each individual word through time from the first written records to the present moment. Words constantly adapt and mutate, influenced by one another and by cultural change. The OED structures each entry according to a complex externally imposed schema of which alphabetising is only the most obvious, but words have internal structures.

Like minerals, words are complex structures generated over time by self-determining rules. I am interested in the possibility of visualising the internal structures within language as a physical manifestation. My choices of material and the placement of each object are governed by rules suggested by the kind of relationship one term in a group has to another. Words are so deeply embedded in our sense of ourselves as individuals and as a society that it can be hard to consider their workings. *Dictionary Ranges* is a kind of word game, an attempt to make the familiar, such as a word like 'table', strange enough to think about again.

Art is extremely well-suited to describing the indescribable and illogical. No other discipline does this so well. It is the tension between the logical system of the OED and the scattered unstable subject of World English that attracts me to the Dictionary. I work with official data sets such as police crime data[1] and the OED because exploitable discrepancies immediately exist between my practice as an artist and the practices that compile the data I work with.

'Everything began with objects, yet there is no longer a system of objects. The critique of objects was based on signs saturated with meaning, along with their phantasies and unconscious logic.'[2] In extremes of complexity, systems of classification break down. By using objects, the complex nature of the relationship between words and their meanings becomes physically manifest. The term 'information fatigue' appeared in 1991 to describe a contemporary phenomenon. The game of super-complexity in art is therefore one to be tested.

1. *Mount Fear*... Police statistics for urban Crimes, 2002 –

2. Jean Baudrillard The Ecstasy of Communication (New York: Semiotext(e), 1988), p. 11.

Dictionary Ranges. Diagram of 'table'
mixed media, 2005, dimensions 2.4m × 1.2m × 2m (detail)

Dictionary Ranges. Diagram of 'table'
2005, installed at the London School
of Economics

Dictionary Ranges. Diagram of 'table' with detail showing 'turn the tables' branching from 'tables' (backgammon) mixed media, 2005, dimensions 1m × 0.5m × 3m

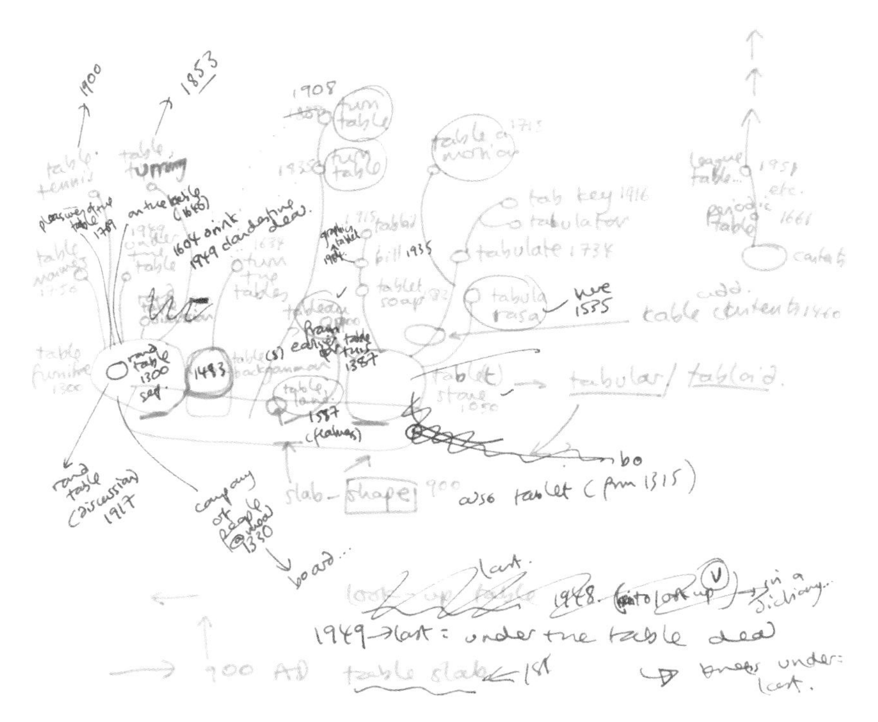

Etymological drawing for 'table'

Adele Prince

Born: 1972
Nationality: British
Lives: London
Title: *Trolley Spotting*
Location: Web-based commission for www.daytodaydata.com
Website: www.trolleyspotting.co.uk

For *Day-to-Day Data*, I am documenting shopping trolleys that have been abandoned (or 'liberated') from supermarkets local to each of the three gallery venues. I am fascinated by the fact that these trolleys manage to travel quite some distance from their 'home' supermarket, and often start to acquire items as they go. The trolleys look quite dejected as they sit at the side of the road, or peep out from behind a tree and I am interested in capturing the different methods of disposal, ranging from careless dumping to considered parking. I would like to determine if trolley dispersal differs in different areas of the country and in different parts of a city. It is something I became aware of whilst living in Islington, where most visitors to the local supermarket walk home with their shopping instead of using a car, so therefore feel the need to adopt a trolley when they exceed a manageable number of bags.

As part of my research process, I am spending time in each of the three cities the exhibition visits, documenting trolleys in the local area. Using a Global Positioning System, I track my journey and the co-ordinates of each of the trolleys I find. For each trolley, I take a photograph, document the model and make of the trolley, the date, time, location and distance from the supermarket. This information is then transferred to an interactive map online, where visitors can go on a virtual trolley spotting walk and play a shopping cart game. Visitors to the galleries can pick up a map that will take them on a shopping trolley tour of their city, taking in trolley hot spots and allowing them to add their own trolleys along the way. Alongside the creation of maps, I am working closely with local supermarkets, tagging their trolleys so that they can be easily identified and to alert people to the fact that they are being monitored.

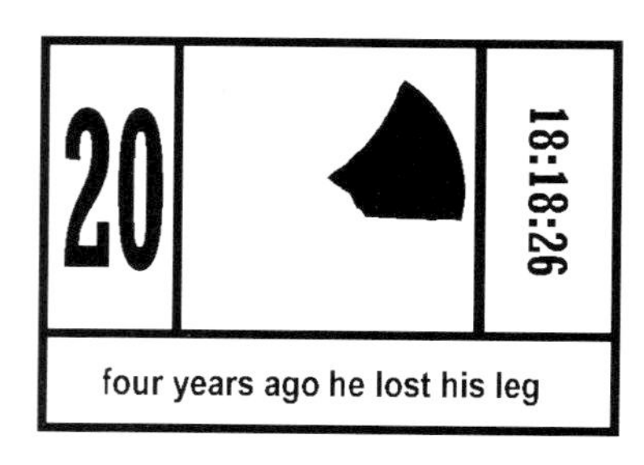

Buko SES100R
Asda
Brougham Road
Portsmouth
23/07/05

Anders Bojen & Kristoffer Ørum

Born: 1976 & 1975
Nationality: Danish
Live: Copenhagen
Title: *Detergent (Real imaginary system)*
Location: Web-based commission for www.daytodaydata.com
Website: www.anders-kristoffer.dk

Gazing deeply into the box of detergent from our local supermarket we see unlimited potential: many systems of knowledge unfold from the qualities of this familiar object, creating almost impossible associations. The pseudo-scientific knowledge with which we are presented, when buying a box of detergent, develops into facts about lasers made of carrots and spinach, and soap bubbles as a new kind of medicine.

We perceive science as a place where the fictional and factual become indistinguishable, and where irrational and mystical knowledge is produced. Our view of science connects with our experience of the everyday and is exemplified through the box of detergent. Its smell, texture and colour are a whole series of sensory experiences. The detergent is surrounded by an entire universe of imagery, such as waves, vortexes, bubbles and whiteness in general. As such it becomes a significant part of the everyday mythology through which we see and understand the world.

Our research is based on what we read on the labels of things in the supermarket, on popular scientific literature and, especially, on the multitude of websites which contain deliberately misleading or misunderstood scientific facts. We want to believe everything, all of the conflicting / alternative visions of the world that these varied sources present us with.

In our laboratory we exchange our eyes for soap bubbles and they feel much better. With soap synapses instead of our organic ones, we are able to observe with a new sense of confidence. We simply help each other pull out our old ones and insert the glittery soap bubbles, caught amidst their graceful flight. Soap bubbles flow freely in our veins crackling as our blood passes from one of us to the other, linking us forever.

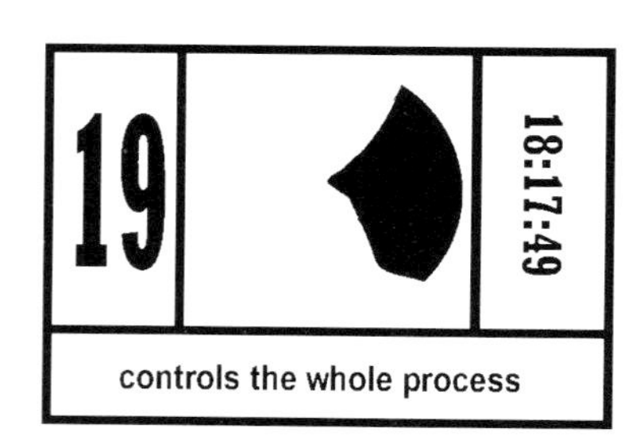

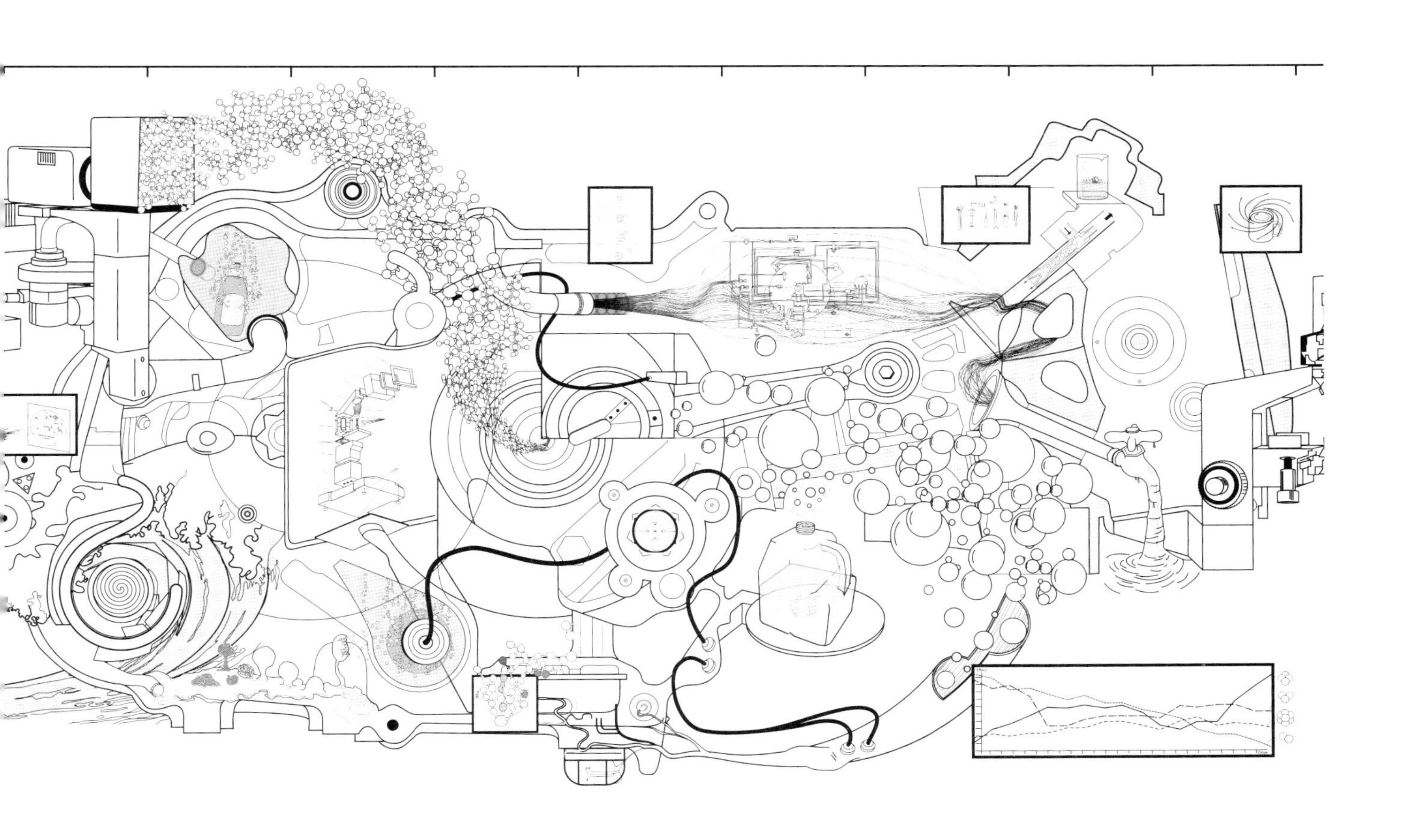

Christian Nold

Born: 1976
Nationality: British
Lives: London
Title: *Bio Mapping*
Location: Available at all gallery venues
Website: www.biomapping.net

Bio Mapping is a tool for gathering biological data about our body. It uses a bio sensor which logs our physiological arousal level in conjunction with a Global Positioning System which locates our position on earth. As you walk around the city, these two devices combine to create personal, emotional maps that record the exact positions of where on earth we feel relaxed or aroused.

The finger cuff sensor records changes in our galvanic skin response which are said to indicate emotional states. The sensor is based on the polygraph or lie detector test but the data recorded is for our own personal interpretation rather then external monitoring.

After returning from their walk the participants see their own *Bio Map* and discuss how it relates to their experience. If they wish, they can share the data of their walk with the rest of the participants in order to construct a communal map that visualises where in the city the group feel most relaxed or aroused.

Bio Mapping is a continuation of the 1960's concept of psychogeography – a personal emotional geography that can be explored and recorded by drifting through the city. *Bio Mapping* extends this idea by providing a way to aggregate this subjective information, creating a new kind of intersubjective data.

Will other people's experiences allow us to engage differently with our environment?

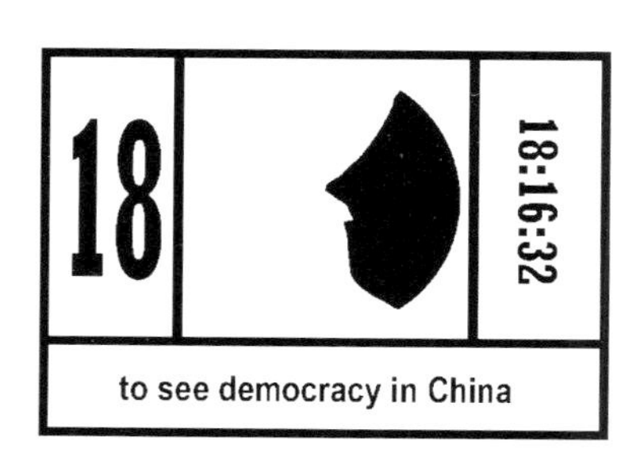

BioMapping

The system got a lock in the park while I was having lunch, and then mapped my route around the Round Pond which was not without incident. Halfway around, a woman walking two dogs tried to help one out of the water and slipped and fell in. Several passersby intervened. The exact spot of the drama was recorded bright red by the GSR device. A little further on I saw someone doing exercises who I thought I recognised, but couldn't see their face. I paused and waited until they turned to face me, and though it wasn't them, I guess the suspense was strong enough to trigger a physical response.

It would be really intriguing to see how my behaviour and my actions in such situations might alter if I had been aware of my own GSR state, but situations were unexpected and absorbing and as such at those moments I didn't register that I was wearing the device.

– Reg's Bio Mapping report, 29th June 2004

pyright. All rights reserved. Nottingham City Council Licence number 100019317 2005

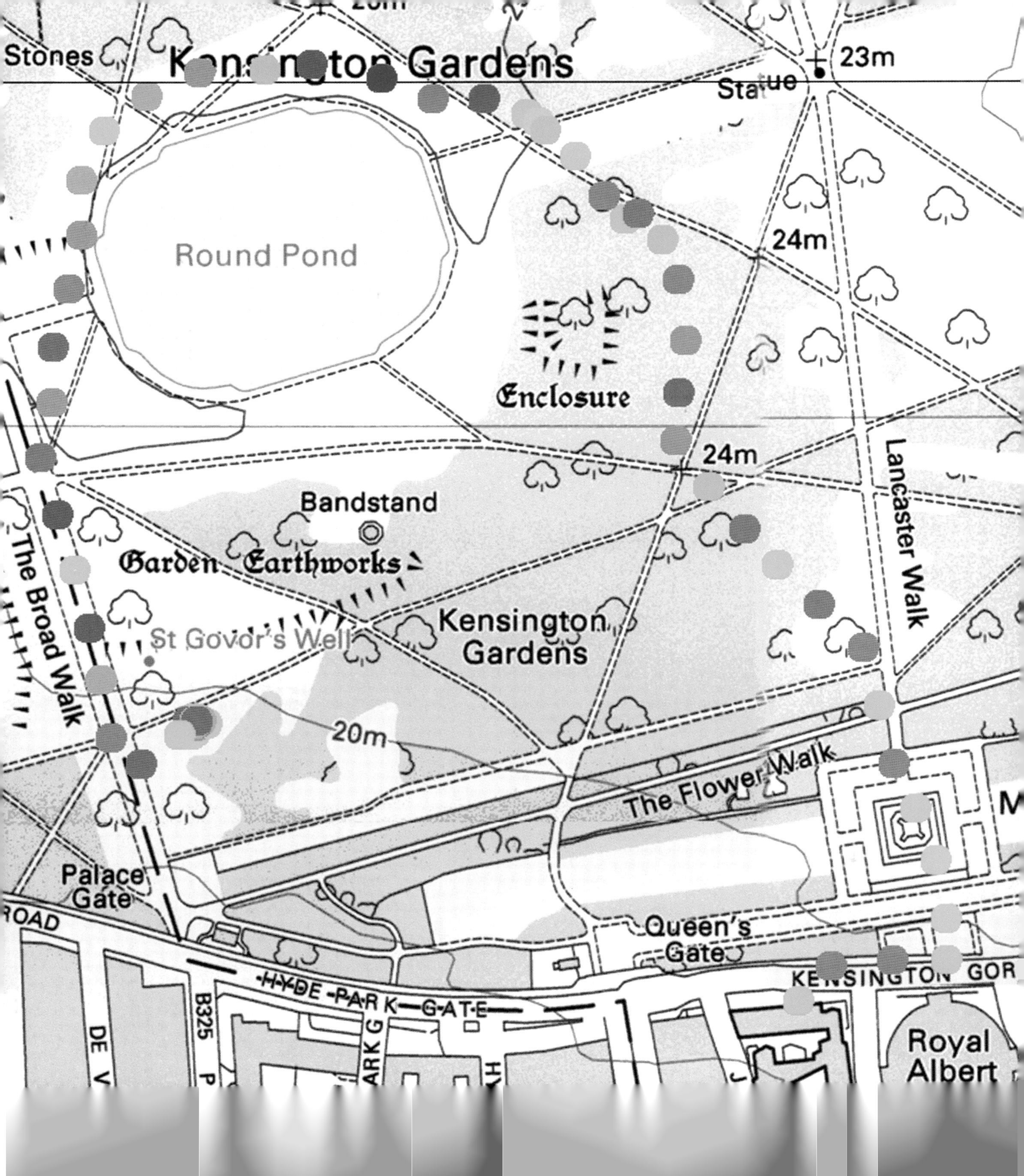
Stones
Kensington Gardens
23m
Statue
Round Pond
24m
Enclosure
24m
Bandstand
Garden Earthworks
The Broad Walk
Lancaster Walk
St Govor's Well
Kensington
Gardens
20m
The Flower Walk
Palace
Gate
ROAD
Queen's
Gate
KENSINGTON GOR
HYDE PARK GATE
B325
Royal
Albert

Cleo Broda

Born: 1970
Nationality: British
Lives: London
Title: *Personal Soft Data Archive System - Objects*
Location: Installation at
Danielle Arnaud contemporary art

In a time when people are encouraged to own more things than ever before, I am interested in the relationship we have with the objects we possess. It is often cheaper to replace an object than to repair it and the renewing of objects in our homes is often more to do with changing taste than with the functioning potential of the object. Consequently, many objects are not made to last. And yet, there is a boom in the 'storage' industry. Many people are paying more to store and preserve objects than the objects are actually worth.

Heirlooms used to carry with them stories of the people who owned them and of the homes they occupied. Because these cherished objects can be triggers for memories, it is often difficult to dispose of them. They may retain this 'memento' function long after they cease to serve the purpose for which they were designed.

The Personal Soft Data Archive System allows people who are attached to objects for sentimental reasons to dispose of the physical objects while preserving their 'memento' value. It functions a bit like microfiche storage for newspapers in that it shrinks the space required for storing the important information. The system stores a visual record of the object but also records any associations the owner has with it. The owner is then free to dispose of the actual object.

It is often the case that minimal living is facilitated by generous, clever storage. This system allows owners to preserve the emotional associations they had with the object while appearing to have a pared down, clutter-free life.

The development of this system is entirely hypothetical and has nothing at all to do with my life or my attachment to teacups or beautiful, but broken, chairs.

Personal Soft Data Archive System – Objects

Outline of a tried and tested system for effectively archiving personal soft data (with special reference to objects which have become obsolete or are broken and yet still function by holding sentimental value).

Context

The System has been developed for those living in societies where:

- objects quickly become obsolete
- it is often more expensive to repair something than to replace it
- pared down minimal living is seen as desirable, fashionable, virtuous and a sign of strength
- heirlooms aren't what they used to be

The System is especially for:

- those with a weakness for possessing things
- those who are predisposed to anthropomorphising objects and imagining that they have feelings and memories
- those who have limited storage capacity: without access to basements, attics, sheds or barns

Aims

- to allow individuals to record what is important for them about an object and to store this information in a (preferably digital) space-saving archive
- to let go of the physical object once the essence of the object is safely archived

Objectives

- to preserve memories triggered by particular objects
- to record the history of the objects
- to dispose of the objects

Method

Follow these three easy steps to freedom:

- visually record the object
- carefully annotate the visual recording with all memories associated with the object
- dispose of the object humanely (those prone to anthropomorphising objects may like to get a friend to do this for them to avoid upsetting image flashbacks and recurring abandonment nightmares)

Advantages of the system

Once the object is destroyed, the annotations may be embellished to exaggerate the object's importance. Since the object no longer exists, future generations will have no way of authenticating the information recorded about the object. This allows the objects to truly function like heirlooms.

Notes to users: In some cases you may find that after recording your associations with an object it is harder to part with it. In this case, it is best to keep the object until you are really ready to say goodbye to it.

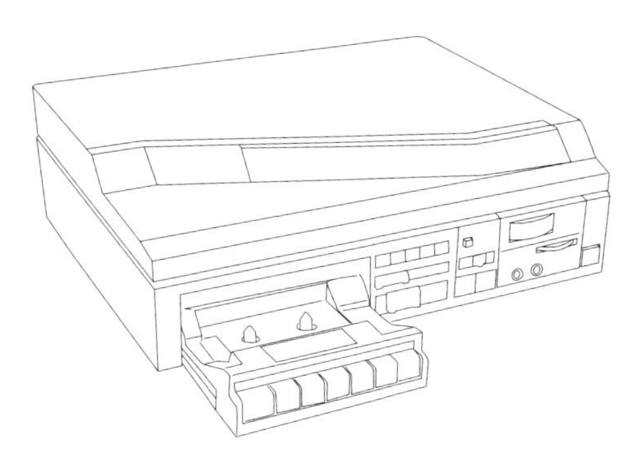

Images from a personal archive

Ellie Harrison

Born: 1979
Nationality: British
Lives: Nottingham
Title: *Daily Data Display Wall*
Location: Installation at all gallery venues
Website: www.ellieharrison.com

Between March 2001 and March 2002 I ate 1640 meals and snacks. Between September 2002 and September 2003 I travelled 9236 kilometres on London Transport. Since 22 April 2002 I have swum 245 kilometres in my local swimming pool. In 2003 I walked 2269 kilometres, drank 559 alcohol drinks, produced 7784 gaseous emissions, read 2185 pages from novels and received 1053 text messages. So far in 2005 I have sworn on 89 occasions[1]...

I can recite all this because for several years I have been religiously documenting small and insignificant events occurring within my everyday routine; experiences most people take for granted each day. Through the act of recording and noting these things down, I have assigned them an elevated status. Immortalising the ephemeral and, over time, building up a vast database of information about my own life.[2] We are all the only true experts on our own lives – I have decided to utilise and strengthen this expertise through my ongoing investigations and the new work produced for *Day-to-Day Data*.

The following pages show the equipment required for the new project. *The Daily Data Logger* is the character I have created to carry out the data collection process. She is an enthusiastic, data-collecting obsessive so keen on measuring / quantifying the things that surround her that she permanently dresses in a tracksuit (for easy manoeuvrability) and wears a utility belt jam-packed with data collecting devices. Throughout the day she records the required information onto the *Daily Data Log* sheets.

This project (unlike previous works) has a live and evolving representation in the gallery space. The *Daily Data Display Wall* is a carefully compiled collection of lights, monitors, sounds, sirens, objects, colour-charts and LED displays which are switched on / off, removed or adjusted, dependant on the data recorded on the *Daily Data Log* sheet and emailed to the gallery each day. The project is intrinsically linked to the gallery as a system and relies heavily on the gallery staff. At the start of each day they must follow the instructions given to reconfigure the *Display Wall*, thereby assisting in the creation of a fluctuating reflection of my own daily life.

1. Correct as of 20 May 2005.

2. All this information is archived at www.ellieharrison.com

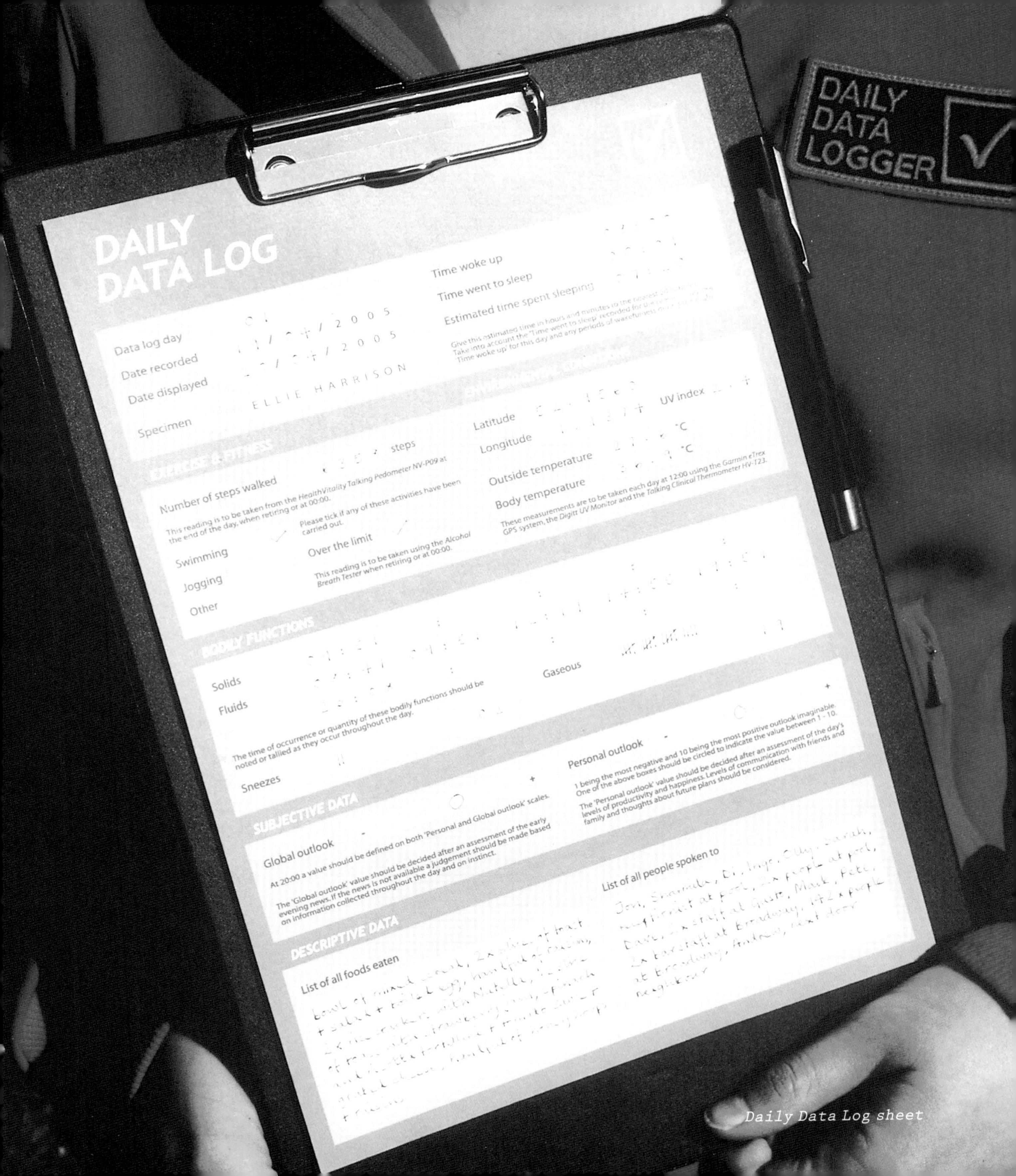

Daily Data Log sheet

Daily Data Logger: tracksuit

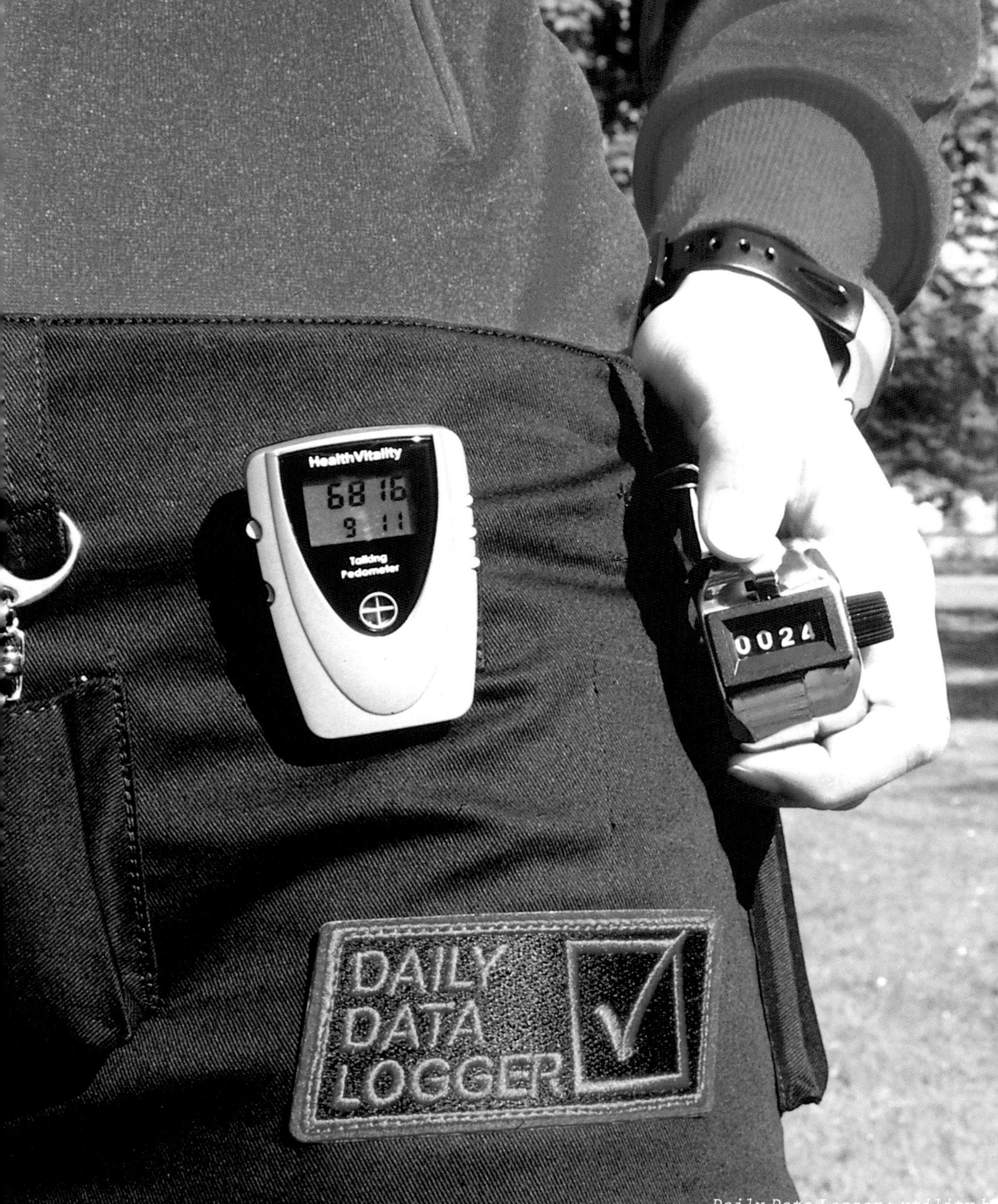

Daily Data Logger: utility belt

Gabrielle Sharp

Born: 1979
Nationality: British
Lives: London
Title: *Losing it in London*
Location: Page-based commission for this publication

This project began after a friend went to Tokyo and lost her diary with her life in it. She went everywhere looking for a lost property office and was told there was none. The diary was lost forever. Their ethos was that if you lose something you can go out and buy a new one; it can be 'replaced'... Money **can** make it better...

Are we different? We as a nation, or so it seems, are emotionally involved with our belongings. They tell a story of who we are. Intrigued by this, I found myself at the Lost and Found Department of London Transport in Baker Street, London and was lucky enough to be taken on a guided tour.

I was astounded by the sheer quantity of lost objects and fascinated to learn that, for the first time in 70 years, the **mobile phone** has overtaken the **umbrella** as the most lost item with 1147 mobile phones and 695 umbrellas being handed in monthly. Intrigued by such statistics, I attempted to document the sense of complete order in what seemed liked utter chaos.

Data protection limits the amount of information you can access from the department and so I began by observing the sorting of the items and the 'ID' procedure which identifies where the item would be held. The process had begun. The ironic thing is that if the items are not catalogued in the correct manner and sorted into the right category, they become 'lost' again within the lost and found department, and are doomed never to be reunited with their owners. It is crucial the items are stored in such a way, which is both efficient of space and time.

It was clear to me that a filtering process was present and this followed right through to the final stage, where the items are stripped down to be sold off or destroyed. I began to see the whole process as a 'cycle', and have broken the following pages into different stages of the 'treadmill'.

over 133,000 items are handed in each year

input

the items come through various transport links and the sorting processs begins

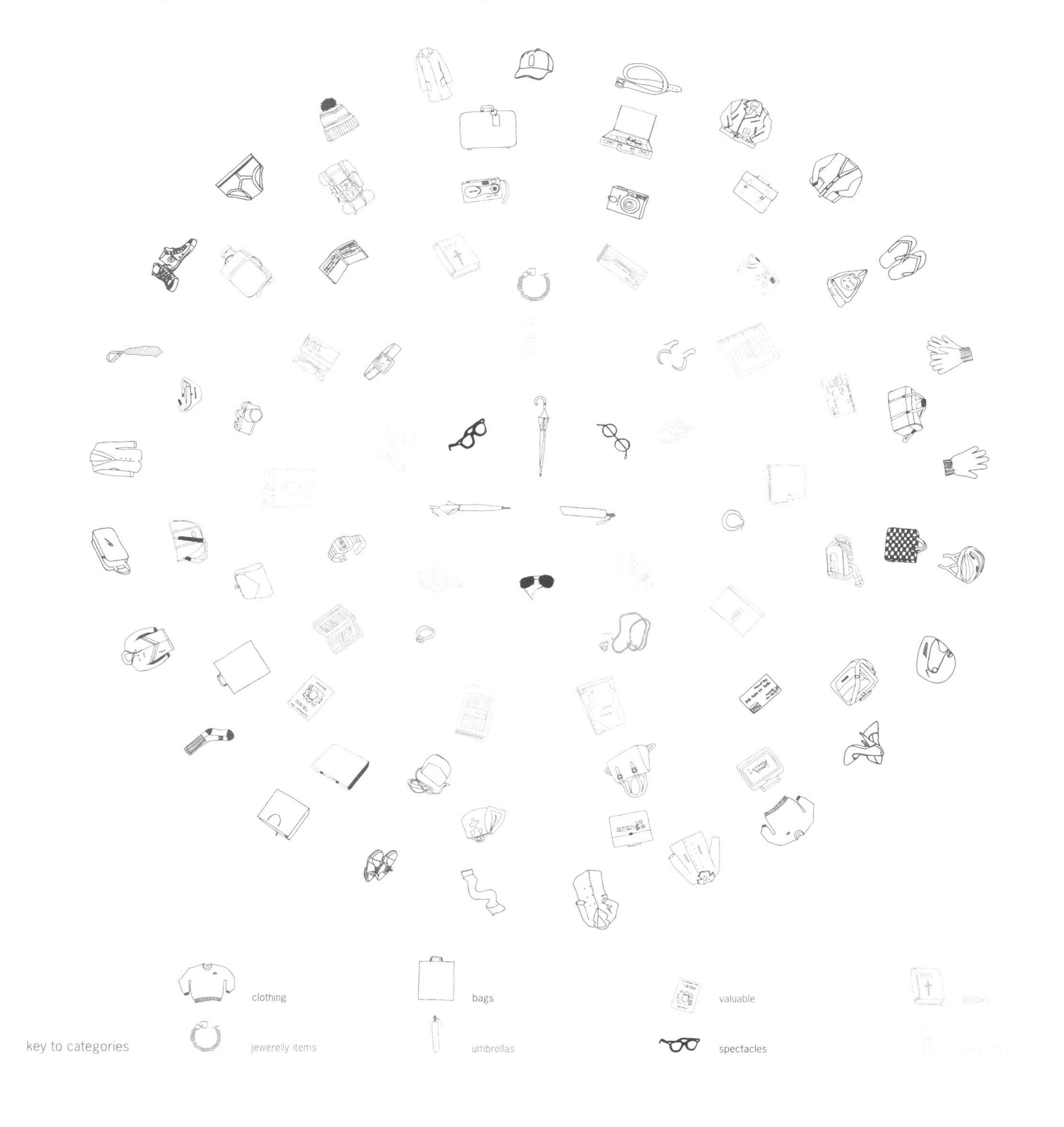

hold

70 phones are handed in each day, that can be up to 25,480 mobiles a year

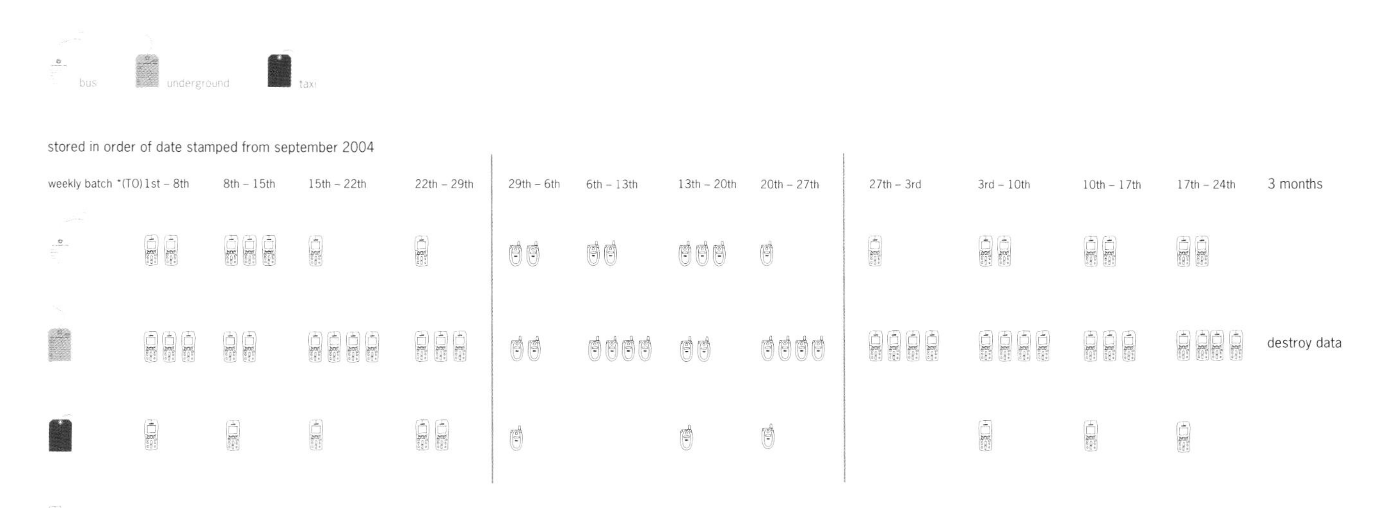

strip

contents stripped for final journey

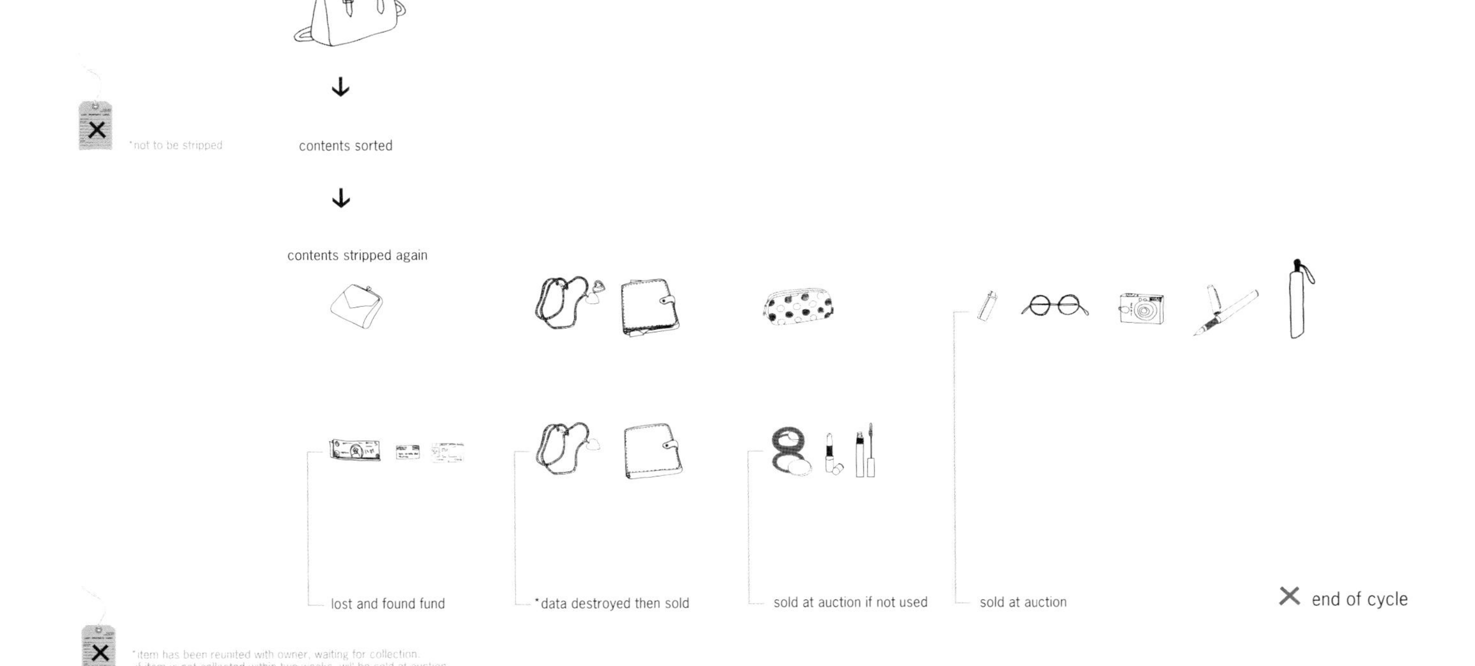

'Not enough hours in the day? Feeling stressed and taking it out on your loved ones? Losing your grip on life? Do not despair; help is at hand! Aided by *DEBASC* you can monitor and develop a successful work / life balance. With a daily and weekly analysis of your emotional profile and task efficiency reflected in easy to read charts it will soon become clear where it's all been going wrong!' *DEBASC* promotional pamphlet.

The *Daily Efficiency and Behavioural Analysis, Self-evaluation Checklist (DEBASC)* was formed as a satire of certain values within British society and the anxieties I experience myself, for work and social ideals. It is designed to be over the top, to the point of absurdity, examining a range of everyday activities. Indeed, the time taken to read the instructions and collect the data would be counterproductive, generating yet another chore – reflecting on the very nature of the checklist's content.

The checklist is broken down into two main sections: efficiency and behaviour. It is then divided into sub-categories and individual tasks. It became clear to me in the production stage that the activities it is designed to scrutinise are in fact the data: my daily routine, self-perception and aspirations are all clearly laid out within the daily 'tasks'. As a prolific list-writer / procrastinator, the taxonomy and design of the check-list took precedence. Whenever I went to fill in the *DEBASC* I was left making changes to the layout or wording instead.

DEBASC is designed to sit somewhere between an organisational skills service and a bureaucratic form. It appears impersonal at first glance. The layout is a fake NHS / Benefits Agency form (with the sentimentality of a 1950's home management guide thrown in for good measure) but on closer inspection it is extremely intimate. This is a highly personalised form, relevant for only a limited amount of time.

Daily Efficiency and Behavioural Analysis, Self-evaluation Checklist (DEBASC)

HB0105/07 – Candidate guidance notes – Examples

SECTION 1 – EFFICIENCY (1E) HOUSEHOLD – tasks: 1E4. Tidy bedroom – general *

* To gain a point for this task the following extensions to the task should also be completed and checked:

(a) Make bed

(b) Tidy dressing table

Daily Efficiency and Behavioural Analysis, Self-evaluation Checklist (DEBASC)

HB0105 / 07 – Candidat guidance notes – Examples

SECTION 1 – EFFICIENCY (1E) HOUSEHOLD – tasks: 1E4. Tidy bedroom – general *

(c) Empty bin

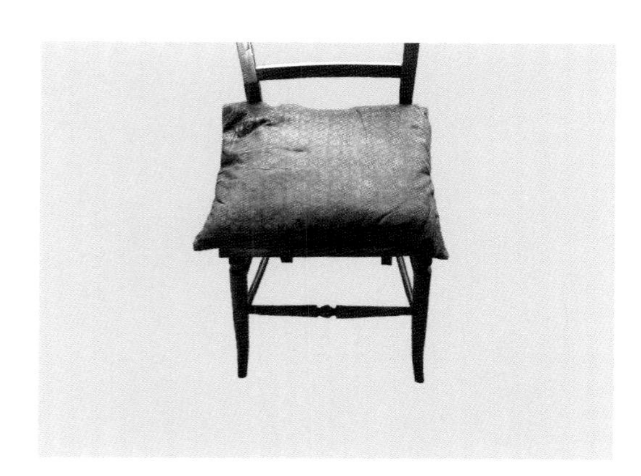

(d) No piles of clothes left lying around

Daily Efficiency and Behavioural Analysis, Self-evaluation Checklist (DEBASC)

HB0105 / 07 – Candidate guidance notes – Examples

SECTION 1 – EFFICIENCY (1E) HOUSEHOLD – tasks: 1E4. Tidy bedroom – general *

(e) No cups or dishes left lying around

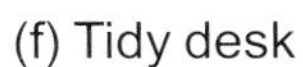

(f) Tidy desk

Helen Frosi

Born: 1980
Nationality: British
Lives: London
Title: *Life / Lotto*
Location: Installation at all gallery venues

Taking inspiration from Socrates[1] and Pataphysics,[2] I have assigned myself the role of the quasi-scientific meddler, whose philosopher's stone constitutes an amalgam, blending scientific principles with all things whimsical and poetic. Through my own particular branch of pseudo-science known as *Quidditology*,[3] I have, by examining the arcane elements of everyday living, formulated a hypothesis for winning lottery numbers...

Life / Lotto came to fruition from my fascination with (subliminal) signs and ciphers hidden within the minutiae of everyday routine. By documenting the tiny nuances and serendipitous events in my day-to-day occurrences, I have created unique divination methodologies: *Chromistry*: of colour / diet, *Khawology*: of coffee dregs, *Klaeddr Prognostication*: of clothing, *Manus Vaticination*: of hand-written notes, *Olfactomantic Dowsing*: of odours etc… Each sure to produce riches.

In my preoccupation with explaining the inexplicable, it is the synergy between life-art-science that stimulates my imagination, taking the everyday into the realms of the 'pata-typical'.[4] I am interested in exploring the breadth of knowledge available to me through the experiences I encounter of the metaphysical world.

Hence, for *Life / Lotto*, I have rigorously monitored, over a period of 13 weeks, a great magnitude of amassed 'codes', each sampled from the happenstance of daily life, and each in need of deciphering. The pure immensity of the data collected has made it a necessity to channel my somewhat obsessional methodology and home in on the myriad flux and shifts of daily occurrence.

Life / Lotto is the accumulation of hypothesis, experiment, computations, collations, and comparisons. Most are prepared through analysis and constructed using the conduit of the invaluable Excel database, Word document and PowerPoint presentation (each a programme found on many computers). I have utilised these tools to set the boundaries of my project: By restricting the permutations of possibility, my divinations gain the potency that only becomes apparent in simplicity.

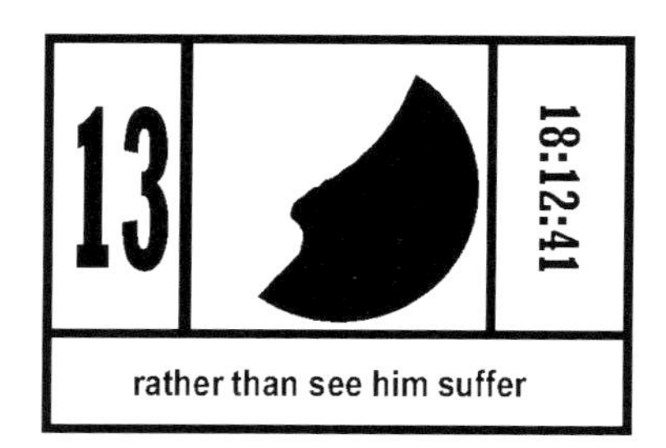

1. Socrates (469 BC – 399 BC) claimed that 'The unexamined life is not worth living'.

2. Pataphysics 'The science of imaginary solutions', founded by Alfred Jarry (1873 – 1907). See: http://home.swfla.rr.com/pataphysician/jarry.htm for more information.

3. The artful divination of customary living: to benefit mind, body and soul.

4. The philosophy or science dedicated to studying what lies beyond the realm of meta-typical. This itself being the study of what lies beyond the typical (or that which is experienced, assumed, customary or normal).

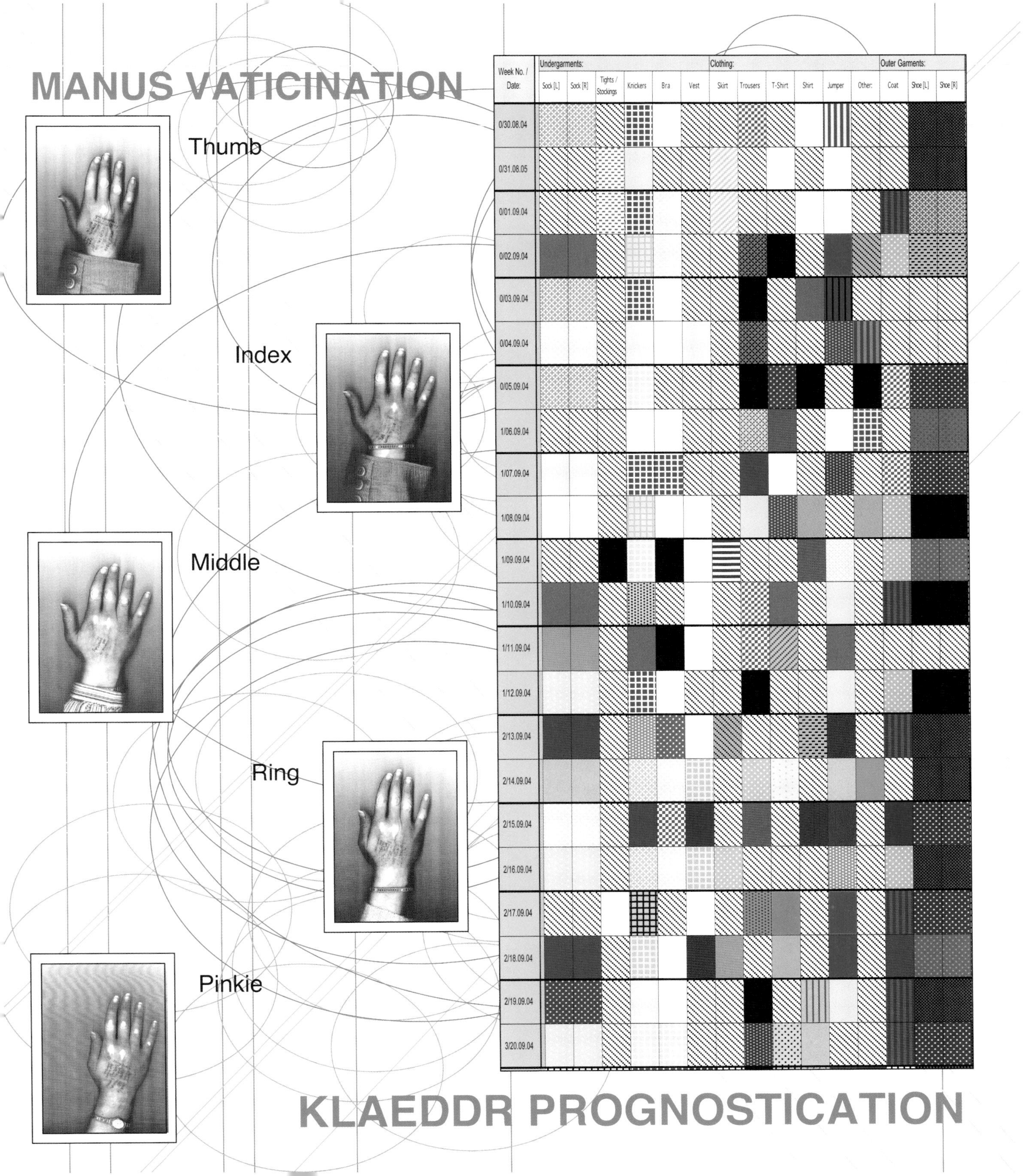
MANUS VATICINATION
Thumb
Index
Middle
Ring
Pinkie
Week No. / Date:
Undergarments:
Clothing:
Outer Garments:
Sock [L]
Sock [R]
Tights / Stockings
Knickers
Bra
Vest
Skirt
Trousers
T-Shirt
Shirt
Jumper
Other:
Coat
Shoe [L]
Shoe [R]
0/30.08.04
0/31.08.05
0/01.09.04
0/02.09.04
0/03.09.04
0/04.09.04
0/05.09.04
1/06.09.04
1/07.09.04
1/08.09.04
1/09.09.04
1/10.09.04
1/11.09.04
1/12.09.04
2/13.09.04
2/14.09.04
2/15.09.04
2/16.09.04
2/17.09.04
2/18.09.04
2/19.09.04
3/20.09.04
KLAEDDR PROGNOSTICATION

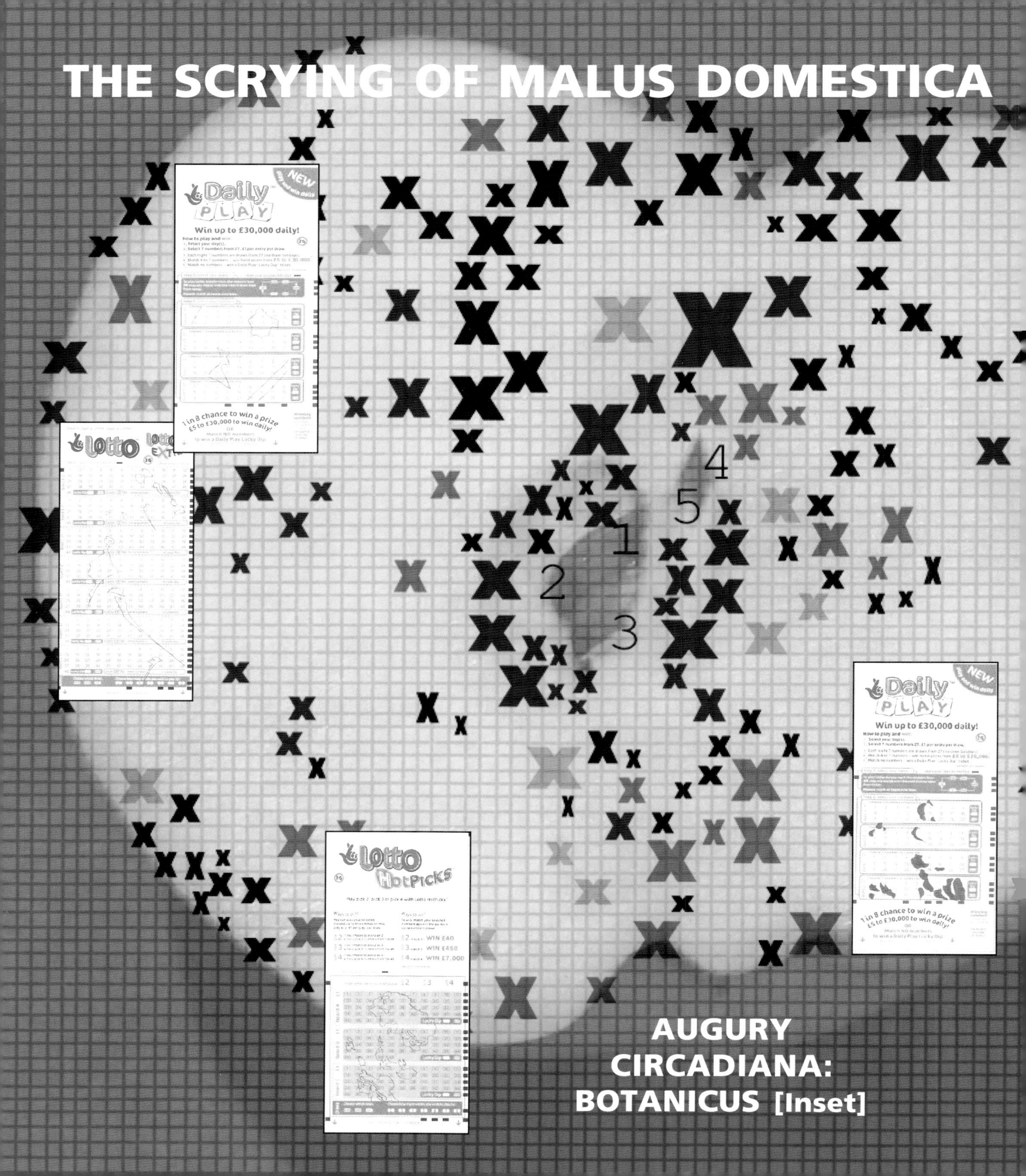
THE SCRYING OF MALUS DOMESTICA
Daily PLAY
NEW
Win up to £30,000 daily!
1 in 8 chance to win a prize £5 to £30,000 to win daily!
Lotto
Lotto HotPicks
WIN £40
WIN £450
WIN £7,000
4
5
1
2
3
AUGURY
CIRCADIANA:
BOTANICUS [Inset]

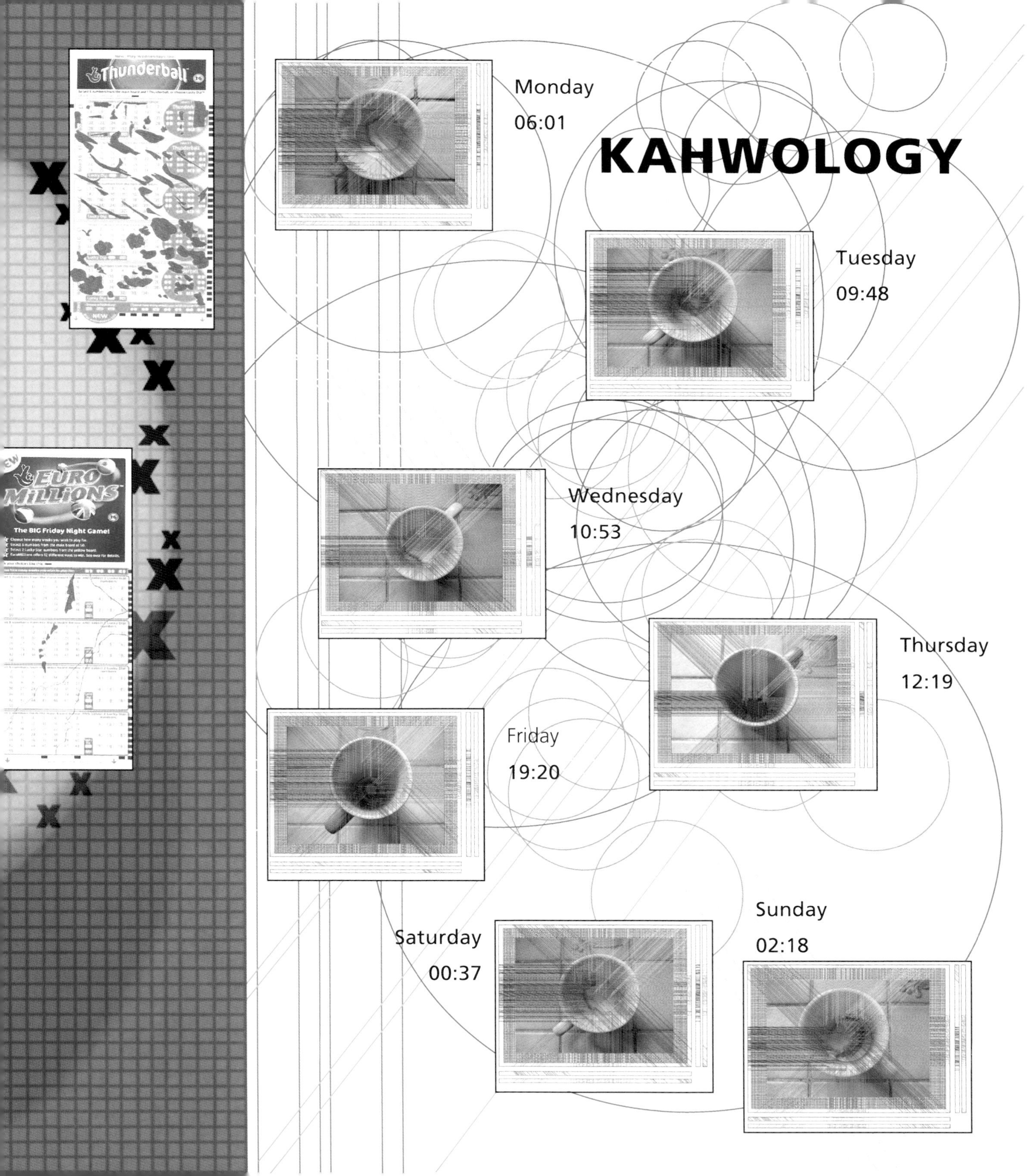
KAHWOLOGY
Monday
06:01
Tuesday
09:48
Wednesday
10:53
Thursday
12:19
Friday
19:20
Saturday
00:37
Sunday
02:18
Thunderball
EURO MILLIONS
The BIG Friday Night Game!

Hywel Davies

Born: 1962
Nationality: British
Lives: Somerset
Title: *Basic Set*
Location: Sound installation at Aspex Gallery
Website: www.hyweldavies.co.uk

Basic Set has grown out of a commission from SCAN.[1] For this project I set myself the task of collecting the same repertoire of sounds in each SCAN location: this included ticking clocks, people humming and counting, and the sound of moving water. This found audio data has already become the basis of short sonic installations in which the data was edited and manipulated before being used as the compositional building blocks within an aleatoric piece.

The principal piece to come out of this project, to be staged by SCAN at a later date, involves the extended abstraction of data beyond the found sound. Each location where water sounds were collected was carefully noted on Ordnance Survey maps, and so acquired a six-figure grid reference. From this data, new musical data (a pitch row) was derived by the six numbers determining the number of semitones between each note. This same numerical data was then used again to determine the note-length and dynamic of each pitch in the sequence (by assigning 10 different note-lengths and 10 different dynamics each a numerical value between 0 and 9). This method is known as *total serialism*.[2] The music derived from each grid reference is further manipulated by presenting different superimposed combinations of the pitch, note-length and dynamic data derived in retrograde, inverse and retrograde inverse forms. In the large-scale piece the music that is derived from each location is played on a different instrument.

All this having been said, this is not the way I normally compose (and therefore does not sound like my work!) – I prefer to explore aleatoric processes and musical instinct. In order to imprint my creative personality on what is simply data, a further manipulation took place.

Basic Set is, if you like, an overture to this larger piece. It presents water sounds collected at each location superimposed with the pitch material in its most basic form derived from the grid reference of that particular recording location.

1. SCAN (Southern Collaborative Arts Network). A consortium of arts venues / organisations in southern England www.scansite.org

2. Total serialism was developed by Messaien, Boulez and Stockhausen, and popular in the 1950s and 1960s.

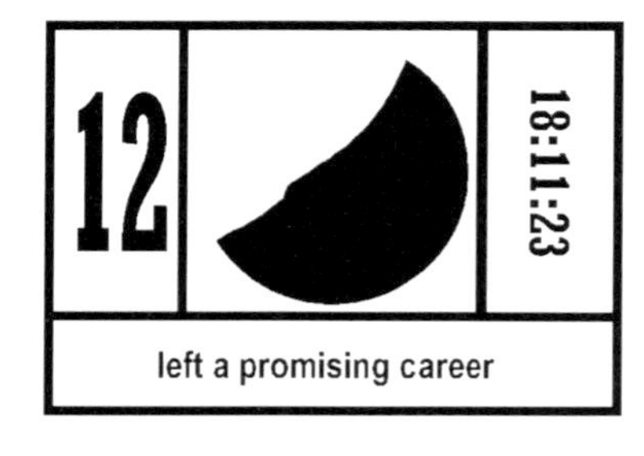

© Crown copyright. All rights reserved. Nottingham City Council Licence number 100019317 2005

The Round House
Crookham Common
WATER
Foxhold Farm
Thornford Road
The Oven
Folly Farm
Swaythling
Mans Bridge
WATER
Riverside Park
Woodmill
Marlhill Copse
Townhill Park
Bitterne Park
SWAY CP
Sway Court
Kings Farm
Flexford Farm
Mill Lane (Track)
Pitmore Farm
Arnewood Court
Hazelhurst Farm
South Sway Farm
Wisbeach Farm
Bowling Green
Bridge Farm
Sewage Wks
Barrows Copse
Erskine Barracks
Chalk Pit
Whiting Works
Quidhampton
Boys Meadow Withybed
QUIDHAMPTON CP
Netherhampton
Oxford Canal Walk
Holman Bridge
Industrial Estate
Spiceball Country Park
BANBURY
ART CENTRE
Manor Farm
Earthworks
Recycling Depot
Grand Union Canal Walk
College
Wolverton
Due to open Early 2004
Organford Manor
Organford Farm
Organford
WATER
Sherford River
Organford Bridge
Caravan Park
Skate Park
IRB Sta (Summer only)
Landing Stage
South Parade Pier
LEISURE POOL
PORTSMOUTH
Pan
Great Pan Farm
ROMAN VILLA (rems of)
Football Ground
Shide
Watch Tower
Pan Down
St Georges Lane
Watergate Road
New Close House
West Standen

James Coupe, Hedley Roberts & Rob Saunders

Born: 1975, 1972 & 1971
Nationality: British
Live: Seattle & London
Title: *9PIN++*
Location: Installation at Aspex Gallery
Website: www.9pinxx.net

9PIN++ is a project that has been very literally 'installed' over the course of 18 months of negotiation with curators, organisations, and committees. It was initially commissioned to map the nine galleries that made up the membership of SCAN.[1] The process involved embedding the project into the institutional fabric of several galleries, including Aspex, by monitoring their activities using a complex system of sensors, actuators and feedback loops. In a way, this is quite similar to the idea of a site-specific artwork, where neither site nor artwork can change independently of the other. With *9PIN++* however, the site was not just a specific gallery but also the network of people, spaces, events and meetings that constituted SCAN. Our aim with this strategy was to have the project's representation determined by its site as much as possible. It looks and behaves the way that it does because that is what and where it has ended up once the component parts of SCAN have been institutionally, politically, technologically, socially and organisationally mapped in relation to the project's aims and goals.

This project was really less about our direct acquisition of data and more about the establishment of a system that would be able to collect data and then autonomously make sense of it. In considering how this would be most effective, we needed to develop an understanding of what would be appropriate for SCAN without ourselves being too deterministic. We wanted the system to discover SCAN itself rather than have us just tell it. A great deal of the process was therefore concerned with making the project as invisible as possible – installing a monitoring system that could co-exist with the normal day-to-day running of the galleries, composing a computer architecture that could evenly distribute the algorithms that we deployed, and responding to the inevitable question of 'what it looked like'. Ultimately, this project is not about visualising data, it is about parasitically installing a system that can use data to understand its host, and communicate that understanding via its actions. The question then becomes 'how has the project changed SCAN?' If it has, then the symbiotic relationship referred to above has been successfully established.

1. SCAN (Southern Collaborative Arts Network). A consortium of arts venues / organisations in southern England www.scansite.org

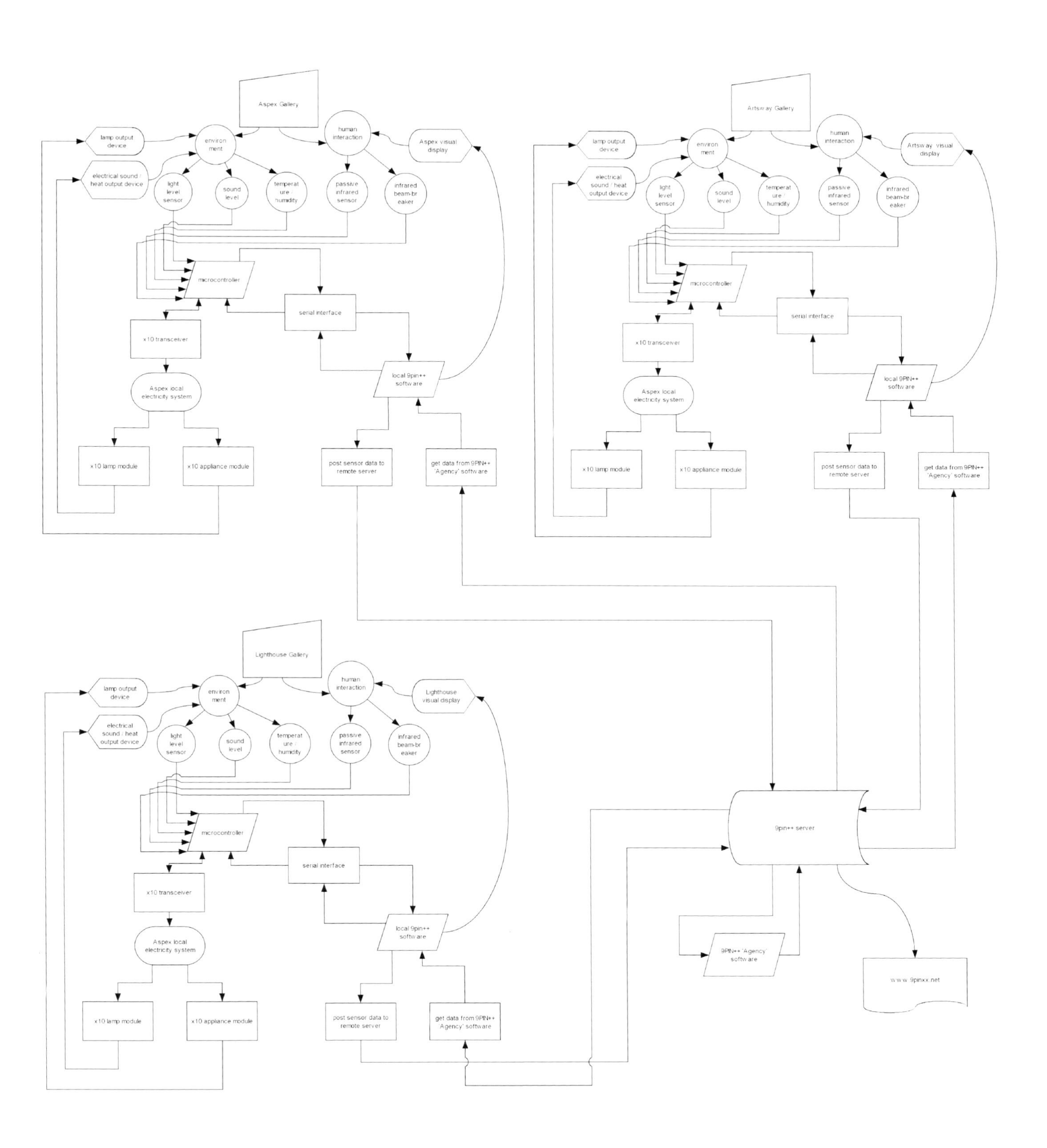

Aspex Gallery
lamp output device
environ ment
human interaction
Aspex visual display
electrical sound / heat output device
light level sensor
sound level
temperat ure / humidity
passive infrared sensor
infrared beam-br eaker
microcontroller
serial interface
x10 transceiver
Aspex local electricity system
local 9pin++ software
x10 lamp module
x10 appliance module
post sensor data to remote server
get data from 9PIN++ 'Agency' software
Artsway Gallery
lamp output device
environ ment
human interaction
Artsway visual display
electrical sound / heat output device
light level sensor
sound level
temperat ure / humidity
passive infrared sensor
infrared beam-br eaker
microcontroller
serial interface
x10 transceiver
Aspex local electricity system
local 9PIN++ software
x10 lamp module
x10 appliance module
post sensor data to remote server
get data from 9PIN++ 'Agency' software
Lighthouse Gallery
lamp output device
environ ment
human interaction
Lighthouse visual display
electrical sound / heat output device
light level sensor
sound level
temperat ure / humidity
passive infrared sensor
infrared beam-br eaker
microcontroller
serial interface
x10 transceiver
Aspex local electricity system
local 9pin++ software
x10 lamp module
x10 appliance module
post sensor data to remote server
get data from 9PIN++ 'Agency' software
9pin++ server
9PIN++ 'Agency' software
www.9pinxx.net

Jem Finer

Born: 1955
Nationality: British
Lives: London
Title: *On Earth as in Heaven*
Location: Web-based commission for www.daytodaydata.com
Website: www.onearthasinheaven.net

To the astronomer stars are data; catalogued, numbered and mapped, graded by size, colour, spectral content and red shift. Their names date back to an earlier age when, ordered into constellations, their passage across the night sky was a clock, a beacon, a calendar for agriculture, a map for navigation, bound in myth.

The stars still hold their mystery and now, millennia after their naming, I wondered where and when these names appeared and how they connected, here on earth.

I soon discovered that I had embarked upon a serious data mining exercise. I imagined initially that all the stars would have streets or towns named after them (or themselves be named after terrestrial locations), but this was far from the case. Using Google as a research tool I found that star names were more often than not the name of an object, a document, a person, something transient at a specific time and place...

Some star names (where they had them) proved so problematic I had to dig far down the line of alternative nomenclature – numbers, Greek letters and abbreviations – to find even one terrestrial manifestation. With others, references were only to themselves or 'useless' data. The star 'Pione', for example, repeatedly yielded typos for the word 'phone'. Eventually, after over 40 pages of results, I found a Pione handbag.

I came across an old atlas and started to draw the constellations onto its pages, layering them on top of the existing maps of data; climate, ocean currents, geology...

Dealing with the ever increasing overload of information, these disparate mappings interconnect nodes on the planet into nonsensical yet ordered networks, into patterns based on the star gazing and pattern forming, myth making past of our ancestors. On earth as in heaven.

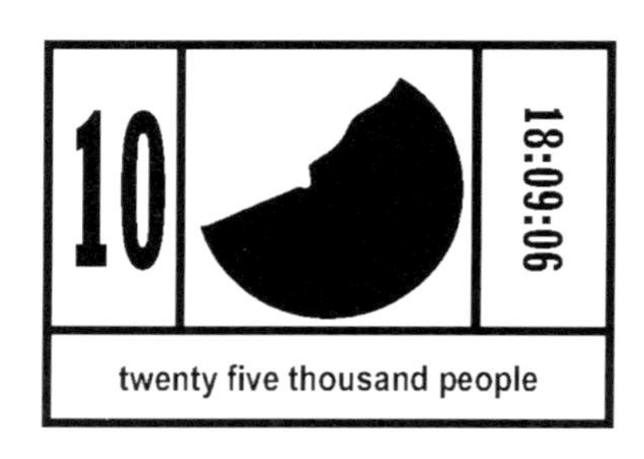

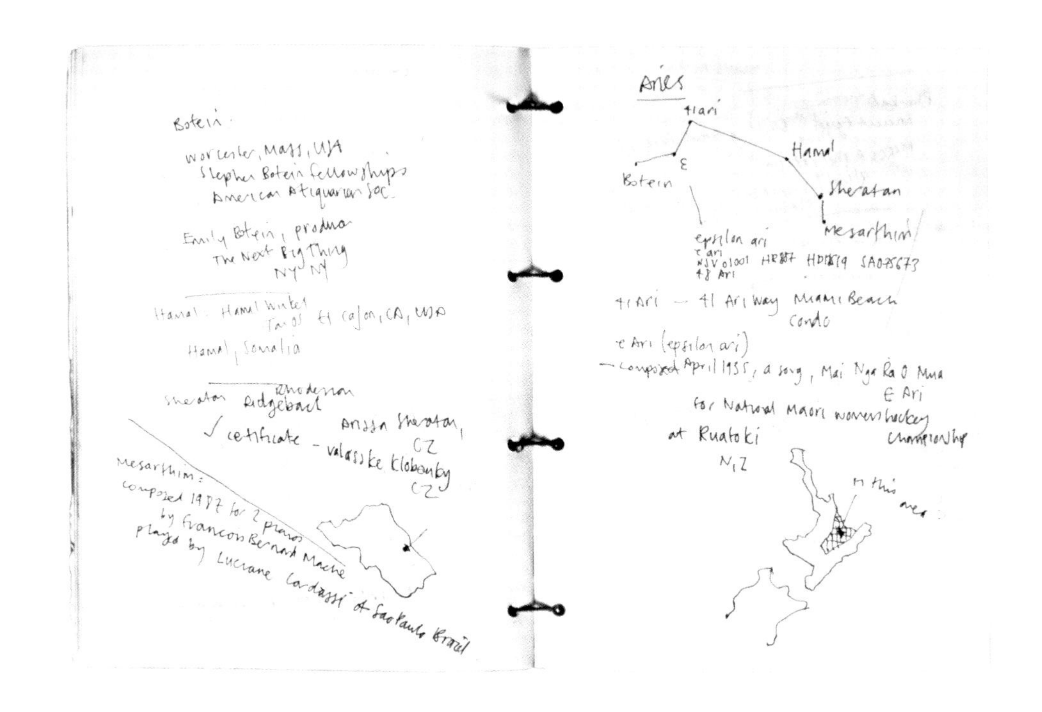

Botein
Worcester, Mass, USA
Stephen Botein fellowships
American Antiquarian Soc.
Emily Botein, producer
The Next Big Thing
NY NY
Hamal: Hamal Wicket
El Cajon, CA, USA
Hamal, Somalia
Sheratan Rhodesian Ridgeback
certificate – Arissa Sheratan, CZ
Valasske Klobouky CZ
Mesarthim:
composed 1987 for 2 pianos
by Francois Bernard Mache
played by Luciane Cardassi of Sao Paulo Brazil
Aries
41 Ari
Hamal
Botein
Sheratan
Mesarthim
epsilon ari
41 Ari — 41 Ari Way Miami Beach condo
ε Ari (epsilon ari)
— composed April 1935, a song, Mai Nga Ra O Mua E Ari
for National Maori women's hockey championship
at Ruatoki
N.Z
in this area

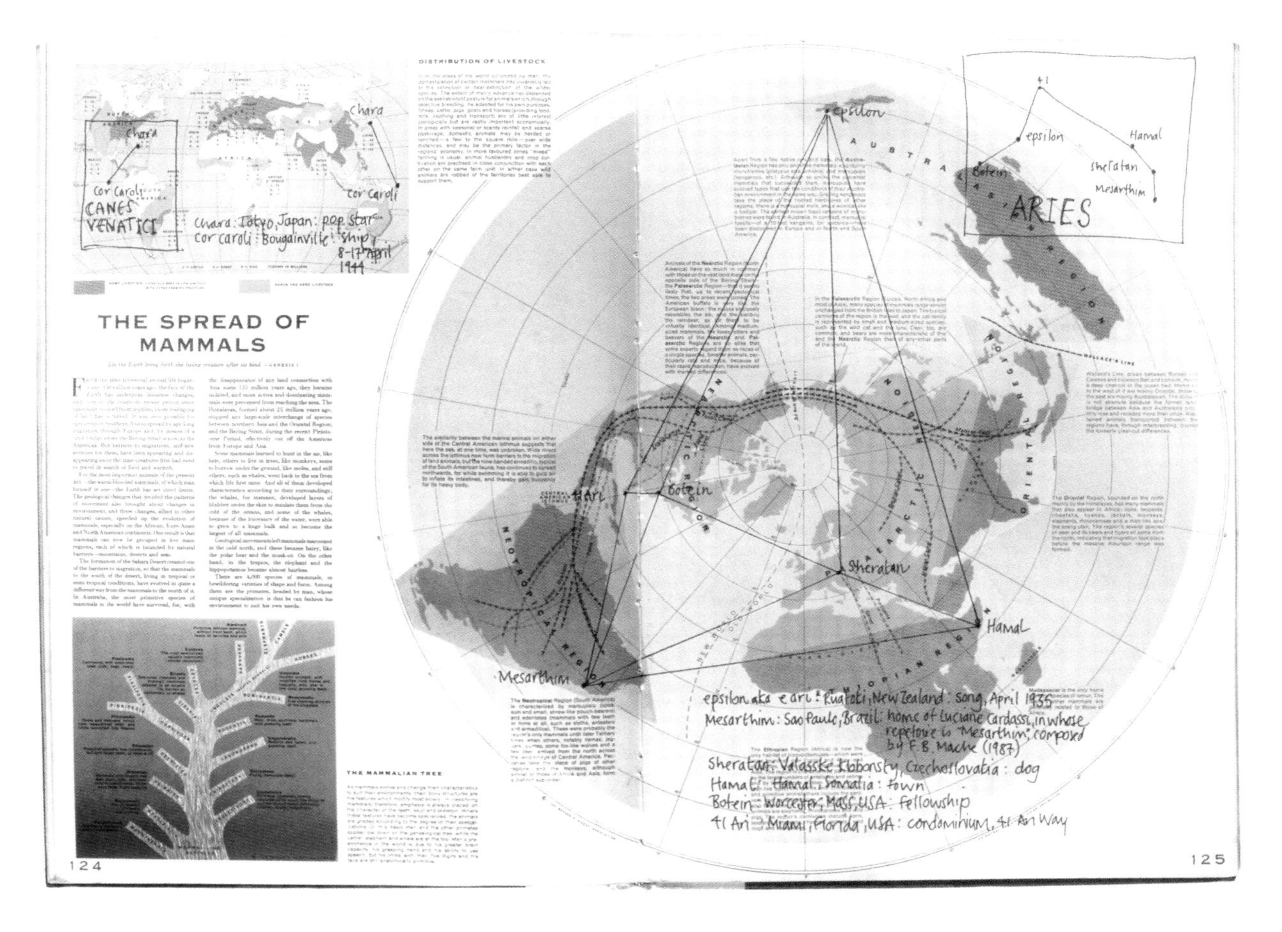

DISTRIBUTION OF LIVESTOCK
Chara
Cor Caroli
CANES VENATICI
Chara: Tokyo, Japan: pop star
Cor caroli: Bougainville: ship 8-17 April 1944
THE SPREAD OF MAMMALS
THE MAMMALIAN TREE
epsilon
41 Ari
Botein
Sheratan
Hamal
Mesarthim
ARIES
epsilon aka ε ari: Ruatoki, New Zealand: song, April 1935
Mesarthim: Sao Paulo, Brazil: home of Luciane Cardassi, in whose repertoire is "Mesarthim" composed by F.B. Mache (1987)
Sheratan: Valasske Klobonsky, Czechoslovakia: dog
Hamal: Hamal, Somalia: town
Botein: Worcester, Mass, USA: fellowship
41 Ari: Miami, Florida, USA: condominium, 41 Ari Way
124
125

Kevin Carter

Born: 1968
Nationality: British
Lives: London
Title: *De do do do, de da da da (They're meaningless and all that's true)*
Location: Web-based commission for www.daytodaydata.com
Website: www.dedododo.com

Much of my work to date has focused on the relationship between society and the utopian promise of technology, in particular the desire for seamless interaction between humans and technology based systems. From a critical point of view this relationship might be understood as a spatial problem, based on a belief that intelligence resides within a technological system, rather than as part of a shared, though often transparent, interaction. It is these interactions, implicit in our relationship with technology, with which my work is currently concerned.

Recent works have used voice, both computer generated and human, as a medium to explore these interactions. Seamless Human Computer Interaction (HCI) is always imagined in Science Fiction to be conducted via the medium of voice. In reality, the current abilities of Speech Recognition (SR) systems fall way short of this fantasy. Current SR software tends to work well in noiseless, context-free environments. But if a particular context is introduced, perception of the meanings produced by the interaction may change radically.

In the manner of SR software architecture, I have compiled a lexicon of words based on my son Jake's pre-language **baby talk**. I have extracted these phonetic **sound words** and their resulting translations from a 7 hour video of Jake's day. These **sound words** and accompanying translations are a guess, made by me, on the articulation and meaning of Jake's words based on the context in which they were spoken.

In parallel to this approach, I was keen to create a particular tension in the way the audiences interacted with the work. The work's interface design and functionality have been informed by *quickfix* language learning resources. This approach is taken to an extreme by allowing the audience to decide how long they wish to spend viewing the work. This decision has an explicit effect on the manner of the work's final representation.

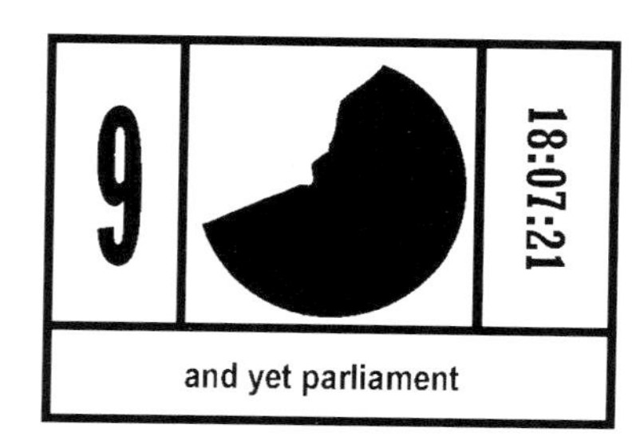

00:00:00:01
00:00:00:02
00:00:00:03
00:00:00:05
00:00:00:16
00:00:00:19
00:00:00:08
00:00:00:10
00:00:00:12
00:00:00:20
00:00:00:29
00:00:01:01

Lucy Kimbell

Born: 1966
Nationality: British
Lives: London
Title: *Untitled (Physical Bar Charts)*
Location: Installation at all gallery venues
Website: www.lucykimbell.com

If there is a subject matter, it is the process of data production and representation. My projects make visible the effects that these have on one another by producing records that are entangled with the things they are recording and their means of production. They seem to show that relations are not external to us – something outside of people or things – but enter into us, and we into them.

In previous projects I have gathered and made public data about myself.[1] I have instantiated data-gathering systems that interfere with a university.[2] I have also designed means that make visible political and citizenship activity.[3] My project for *Day-to-Day Data* ties consumption to data production and representation. What you take is what you see.

Often deploying or undertaking research, my ways of working can resemble management initiatives or social science, in most cases a flawed or failed version, spawning bastardised methods and methodologies, tools and techniques. There are barely research questions let alone answers. In each project I have to work out what can be asked. I must work out the relationship between myself, the viewer, and what can be known. I have to work out how to find out what I believe can be known. For *Day-to-Day Data*, I am asking questions about research by prompting people to think about how they idle away their time in public spaces. The project involves making records that tell us something about relations between people and people, and people and things, and things and things. Viewers consume the piece by consuming part of it. The piece says 'Let us be part of each other'.

1. *Audit*, 2002; *The LIX Index*, 2002 – 2003

2. *Making a Difference at the University of Plymouth*, 2004

3. *Pindices*, 2005, a collaboration with sociologist Andrew Barry

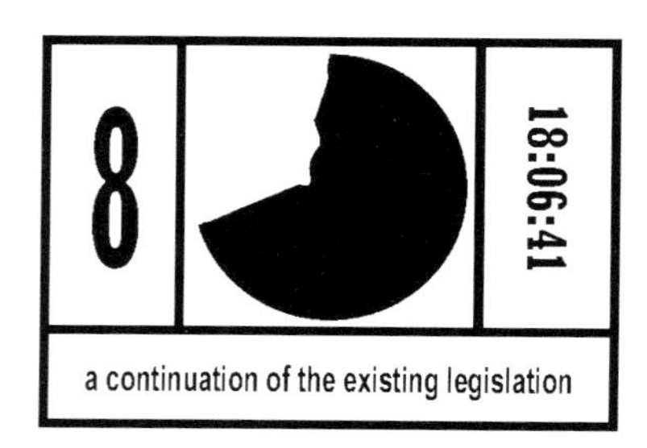

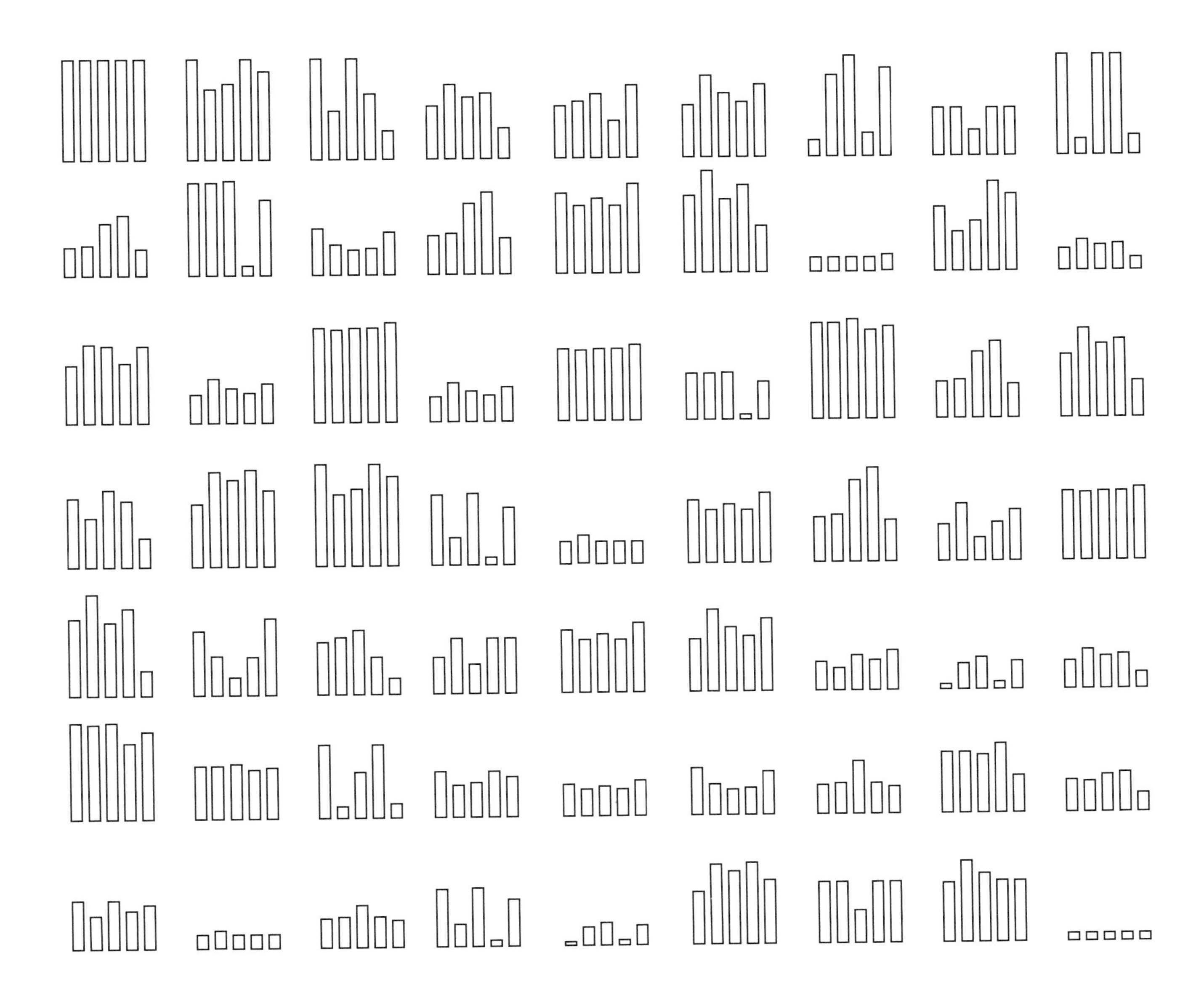

Your data are vital because they have implications for town planners, council service providers, birds, bus drivers, media buyers, shareholders, graffiti artists, underage couples, Tory think tanks, OAPs, sociologists, urban foxes, school children, 4x4 drivers, slobs, mobile phone operators, teenage mothers, consumer electronics product managers, idlers, poster designers, architecture students, pushchair manufacturers, people in search of work, ethical shoppers, flashers, out of town store buyers, bus company managers, Kurdish asylum seekers, drug dealers, musicians, journalists, dogs, muggers, headlamp manufacturers, paedophiles, flower sellers, refuse collectors, vandals, people in wheelchairs, teachers, experts in regeneration, historians, people in search of inspiration, software applications, lesbian women, ants, newspaper vendors, Goths, non-smokers, self-harmers, oil traders, Lacanian psychoanalysts, jogging nannies, buy-to-let investors, forensic analysts, dog walkers, people in a hurry, software designers, police officers, call centre operators, nurses, writers, guide dogs.

I spend my time watching
other people I spend my time
designing improvements to the
house opposite I spend my time
sending text messages I spend
my time reading I spend my
time looking at the crap on the
ground I spend my time eating
I spend my time coughing
I spend my time feeling anxious
I spend my time thinking about
my bills I spend my time fiddling
with my hair

Mary Yacoob

Born: 1975
Nationality: British
Lives: London
Title: *Trace Elements*
Location: Page-based commission for this publication

The following drawings consist of maps of surfaces that reveal signs of human presence in the domestic sphere. Actions that form part of our daily habits and routine, leaving behind clues that can be traced and recorded. The dust, partly formed by our skin cells, that clings to all surfaces, or the disruption of bedcovers after taking an afternoon nap, are signifiers of transformation that form part of our evolving landscape. My work investigates how diagrams and maps – usually used to create universal reference guides – can be used to notate these ephemeral occurrences. In this way, I explore how recording the details of everyday life can intensify our experience of that which is deemed ordinary or disclose obscure narratives.

Tracing an activity has several stages: discovering a scarcely detectable process; observing its development; making a mark; and creating a record. At the same time, counting, measuring, and classifying may reveal a rhythm or pattern at work. This kind of intense scrutiny of the mundane can elicit a sense of the uncanny.

Perhaps our instinct to order and classify stems from our struggle to make sense of the stream of information, memories and experiences which we are subjected to on a daily basis. We develop systems as a kind of coping mechanism. They enable us to relate to the world via filtering processes. Though focused, these systems will always be fragmentary and provisional.

I am interested in how appropriating scientific ordering systems into an art context calls into question their use in the drive for timeless objectivity, and instead brings into play ambiguity and subjectivity. Rather than using them to establish proofs, ordering systems can be used as frameworks within which to observe and describe the poetic in the everyday.

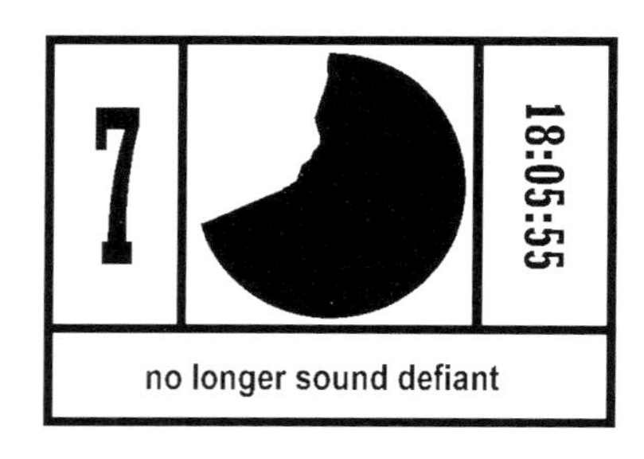

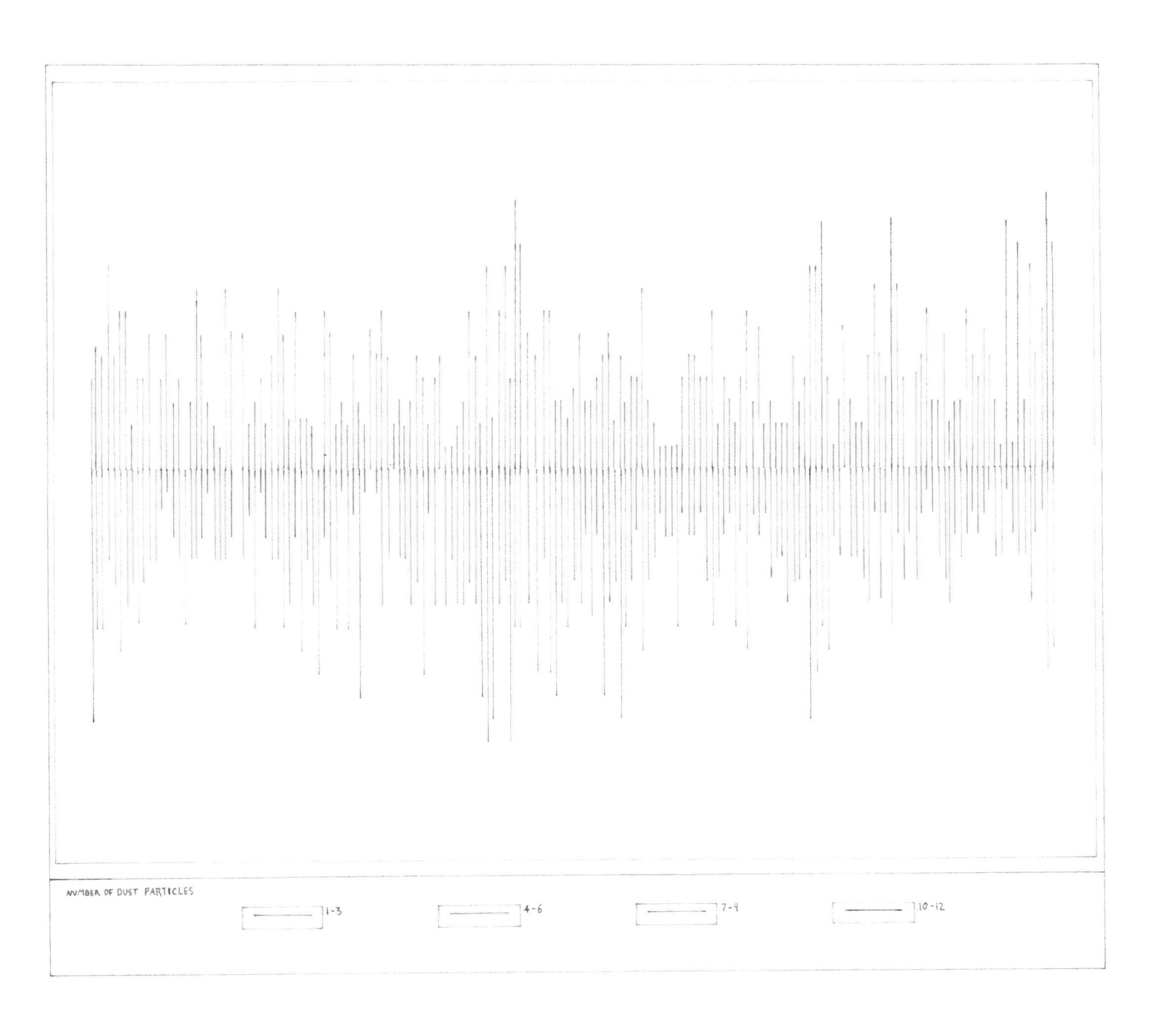

Number of Dust Particles on Television Screen After 24 Hours

Height of Curves in Duvet Cover After an Afternoon Nap

SIZE OF TOOTHPASTE FLECK IN M/M

0.5 1.0 1.5 2.0

Number and Size of Toothpaste Flecks on Bathroom Mirror After Brushing Teeth for 3 Minutes

Richard Dedomenici

Born: 1978
Nationality: British
Lives: Watford
Title: *Nail Salon Belt*
Location: Installation at
Danielle Arnaud contemporary art
Website: www.dedomenici.co.uk

In 2001 I began a walk around the border of the 020 7 inner-London and 020 8 outer-London telephone code areas. I ascertained my route by noting the telephone numbers on shop signs, in phone boxes and by knocking on people's doors. I noticed a higher than average concentration of Nail Salons along the route, and although my walk remains incomplete – partially due to the writer Iain Sinclair stealing my thunder by walking round the M25 – I have developed a theory that, at a certain radius from the centre of London, a *Nail Salon Belt* exists.

In the same way that the Van Allen Belts – bands of ionised gas surrounding the Earth – protect our planet from harmful radiation, I hypothesise that the *Nail Salon Belt* is all that prevents my hometown of Watford from getting sucked into the urban sprawl of London. However, concerns exist that the high frequency of Nail Salons on the border of 020 7 / 020 8 are economically unsustainable, and that erosion of the *Nail Salon Belt* is inevitable. The recent reclassification of Watford Station by London Underground from 'Zone 6b' to 'Zone 6a' seems to suggest that such damage could already be affecting London's pull on Watford.

Urgent data must be collected to prevent imminent disaster. Hence for *Day-to-Day Data* I propose a comprehensive survey of the *Nail Salon Belt*...

Initially, my intention was to collaborate with a programmer to develop an automated 'bot' to trawl business directory data held on www.yell.com, and combine it with the mapping power of www.streetmap.co.uk to generate automated *Nail Salon Belt* data which could then be streamed in real-time into the gallery space. However, for logistical reasons, data will instead be manually gathered and displayed using some little flags, a big map, and a copy of the Yellow Pages.

Nail Salon Belt is the first project I have undertaken which combines geographical mapping and cause and effect. Previous works include successfully disproving Chaos Theory by dressing up as a butterfly in New York, and a failed attempt to turn back time in Central London by travelling anticlockwise on the Circle Line for 43 hours. I'm currently undertaking a study into the feasibility of blowing up the moon.

Didn't expect to be in such a rural kinda place; I was in Hendon five minutes ago. I have no idea where I am and it's getting dark. The only sounds are crunching leaves, birdsong and passenger jets. My map-reading skills no longer come into play coz it's just a green splodge. I walk downhill following the river. Now I am standing in a big puddle, a Glastonbury '98 style quagmire (minus the Stereophonics, thankfully). Ah, an Alsatian: if it comes to it, I can kill it and eat it. But then the owner shows up and looks very terribly posh, so I am too working class to kill his dog. Try to woo a squirrel with some Fruit & Nut chocolate with all the fruit and chocolate bitten off, but he's having none of it.

Sam Curtis

Born: 1981
Nationality: British
Lives: London
Title: *IDUK*
Location: Performance at all gallery launch events
Website: www.scurtis.co.uk

'Citizenship suggests we should be involved in improving society. However, in aspiring to be the dream citizen and undertaking a gigantic bureaucratic task for the benefit of society, Curtis is actually viewed as a nuisance by the authorities and they remain sceptical and untrusting. Although his plan is ultimately flawed, it comments on our problems with the increasing value of personal data and on the alarming methods of identification that are rapidly infiltrating our daily lives. By committing himself to the collective, this unsung hero raises the question of how individuals and the authorities see their roles in society and their relationship to each other.' Citizen's evaluation.

I am on a quest to single-handedly count and record the personal data of all the people living in the United Kingdom. In doing this I will resolve our identity fraud and national security issues. In response to the Government's proposed identity card scheme I have developed my own – the Identity Badge. It is effective, will not be costly and is not obtrusive fashion-wise.

My scheme works by replacing the identity card with a uniquely numbered badge which is presented to each person I count. Their personal data is recorded on a registration form which will be stored until I donate all the data to the Home Office. The Home Office has been notified of my aims.

Included on the registration form is a biometric in the form of a fingerprint. Other biometrics such as iris scans and facial mapping are starting to be more commonly used but I believe fingerprinting to be the most effective and safe biometric for regular recognition procedures. I look forward to counting you and I am grateful for your co-operation when we meet…

Identity Number
Mr/Mrs/Miss/Ms/Other

Therese Stowell

Born: 1965
Nationality: American
Lives: London
Title: *Emotional Stimuli and Responses Over 24-Hour Period*
Location: Page-based commission for this publication
Website: www.theresestowell.com

In order to create a self-portrait of myself as an emotional organism within an ecosystem, I decided to record all of my emotions and their causes for a 24-hour period. I wanted to discover my own predispositions and neuroses, and how my environment shapes my emotions. Does one particular emotional state dominate my day? Or one particular emotional trigger? Am I petty? Judgmental? Do I obsess? How does London impinge on my existence? The form the project takes – charts and diagrams – extends my practice as it quantifies and analyses inherently nebulous data and somewhat absurdly applies objective tools to the subjective.

To collect the data, I kept a notebook with me all day. I intentionally chose a day when I'd be going into the centre of London. As I felt something, I wrote it down along with what triggered it. Sometimes I had to catch up a bit later. The data was intentionally quite raw, and I made sure I didn't edit myself to appear more attractive. Gaps in the day represent emotional drift. Later I tried to impose a rigour on it, transferring it to a spreadsheet to quantify and analyse it. In order to present the data I found I needed to generalise, to flatten the specificity and texture of an emotional response, e.g. pleasure from a short checkout line at the grocery store becomes equal to the pleasure of a phone call from a close friend. The resulting pie charts and bar graph have an opacity and factuality that hide the messiness of me in my world. The diagram presents me as the centre of that world and reveals a bit more, particularly as the raw data sits in the background.

Analysis of Emotional Stimuli and Responses Over 24-Hour Period

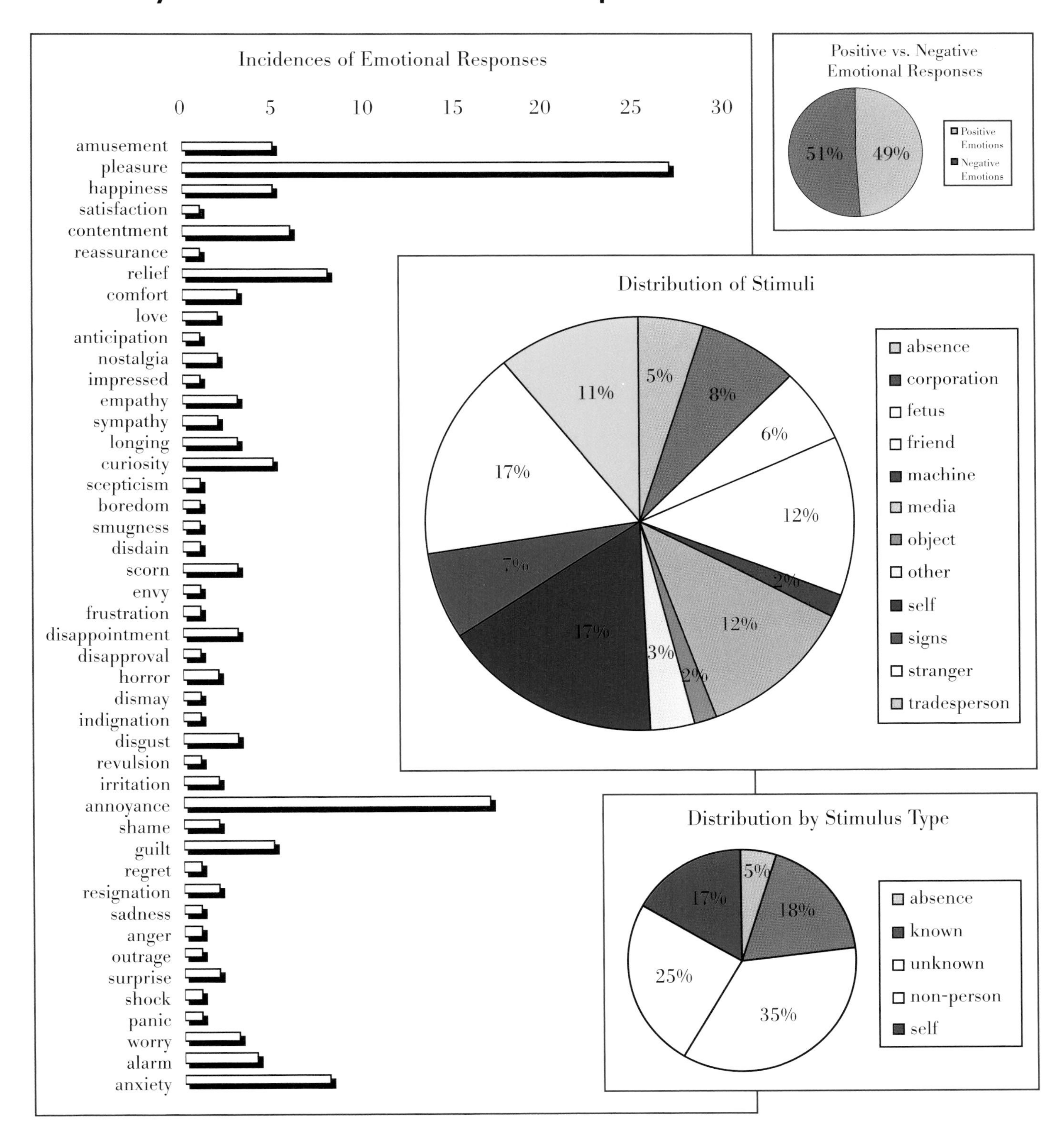

Diagram of Subject w

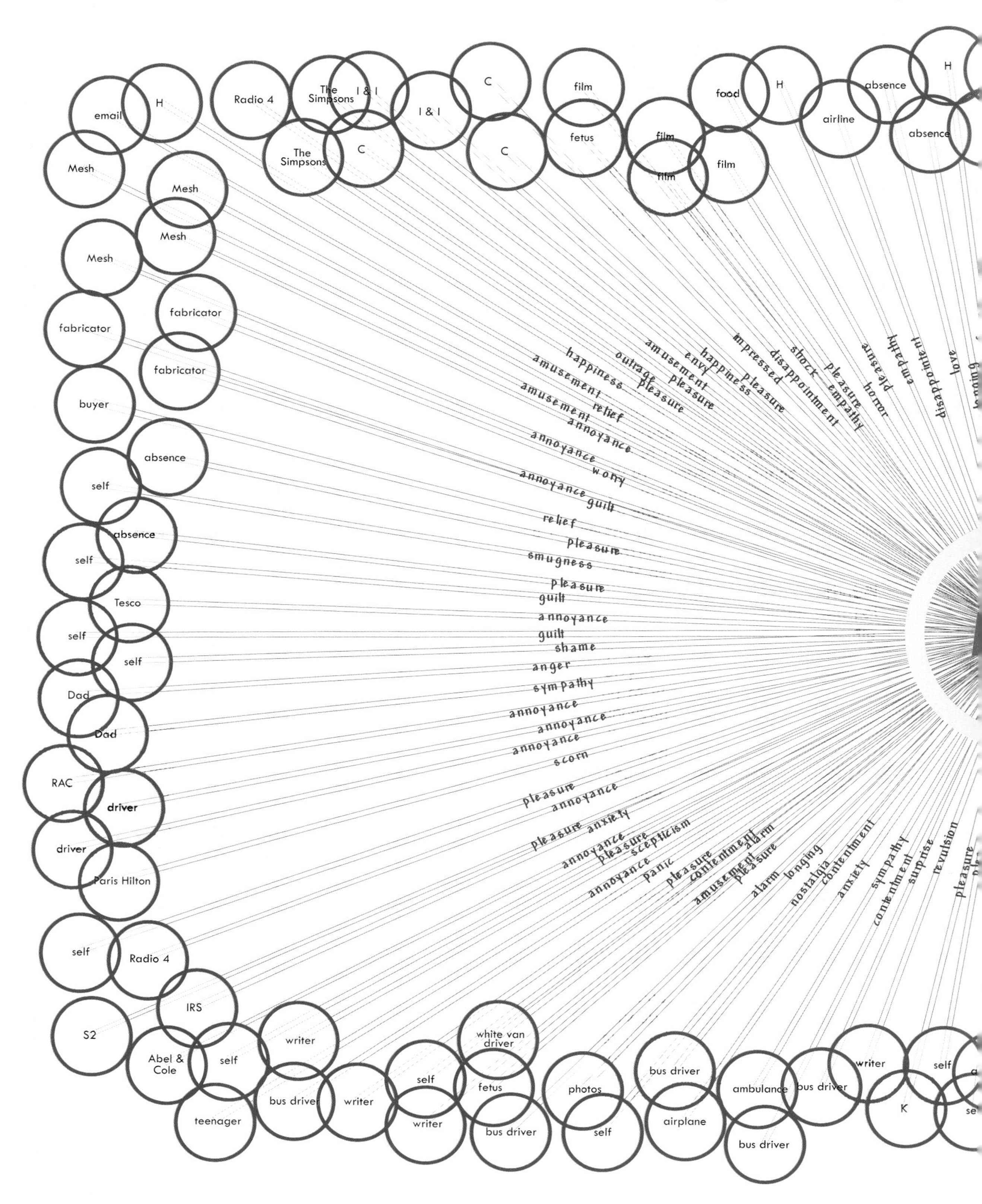

otional Stimuli and Responses

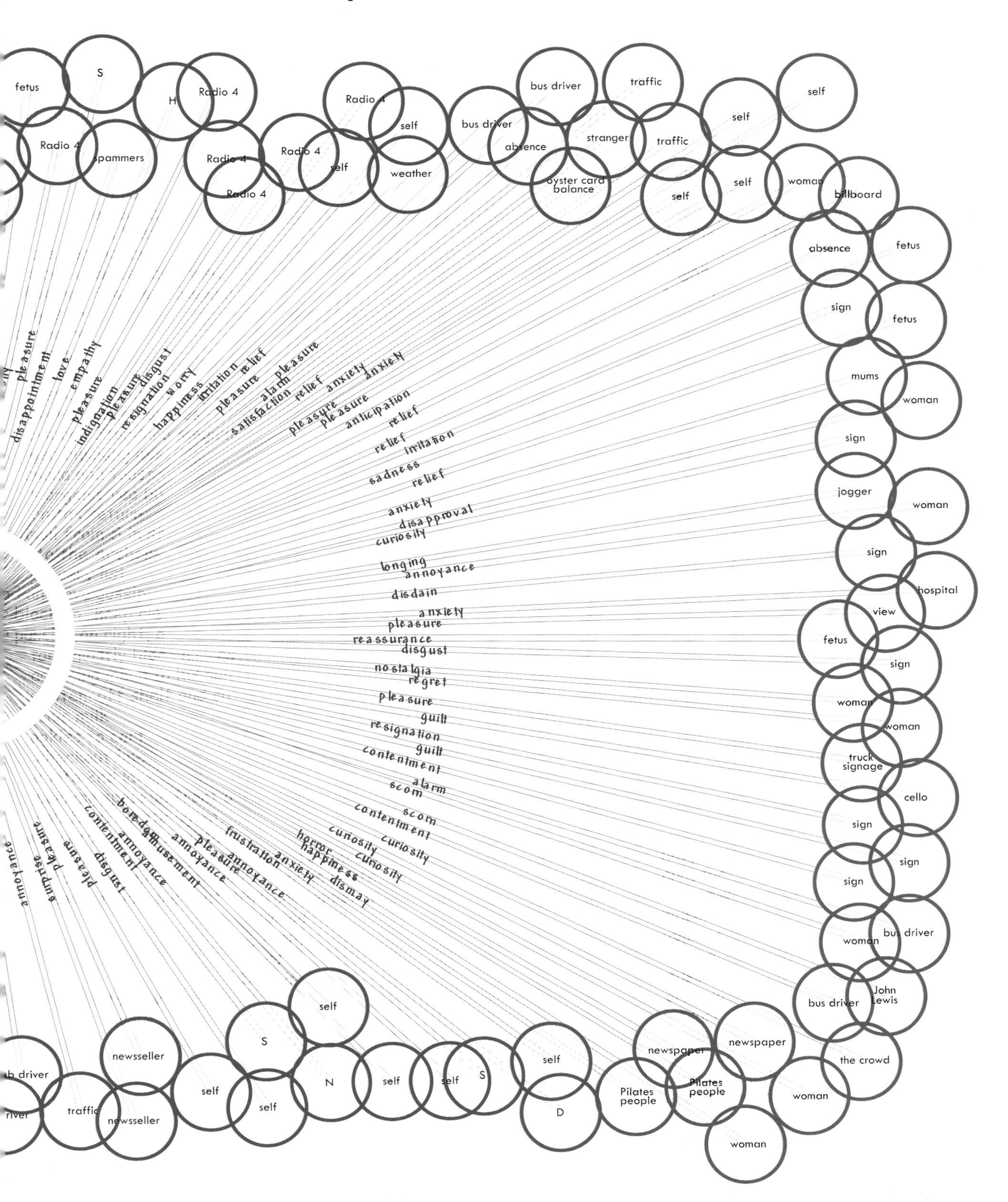

Tim Taylor

Born: 1970
Nationality: British
Lives: Edinburgh
Title: *Our Daily Drugs (Morning Action Patinas)*
Location: Page-based commission for this publication
Website: www.timgtaylor.com

Get up, get washed, get dressed, make a cup of tea. Most British people perform this sequence of events every day, if not necessarily in that order. The daily ritual of the morning cup of tea is an intrinsic part of the British way of life. Furthermore it is one of the more common and widespread practices indicative of the natural disposition of human nature to seek out mental and physical stimuli. Whilst in other cultures the act of tea making is given overt deference through ritual, it is an act that we generally take for granted. It is this act that I wanted to acknowledge and celebrate.

How to celebrate this daily act? What is it a tea bag would like to do once it has fulfilled its reason for creation other than ending up in the bin, or sitting around on the end of a spoon until it is time to wash up? 'Splat!' seemed like the obvious answer. Every morning for a fixed period of time, following the making of my morning cup of tea, I dropped the used teabag from a height of 8ft on to a sheet of paper, thereby interrupting its passage to the bin. I then added the time and date of dropping. In this way the work become a daily record of a fixed point in time within my daily life. Sundays were invariably missing (tea being replaced by coffee) and Saturdays were often recorded later than usual, and with a noticeable difficulty to keep the point of landing to the centre on the paper. The title *Morning Action Patina* alludes to the time of creation, the role the act of dropping plays in their creation and to the use of tea to give works of art a false patina.

Splat! on the paper.

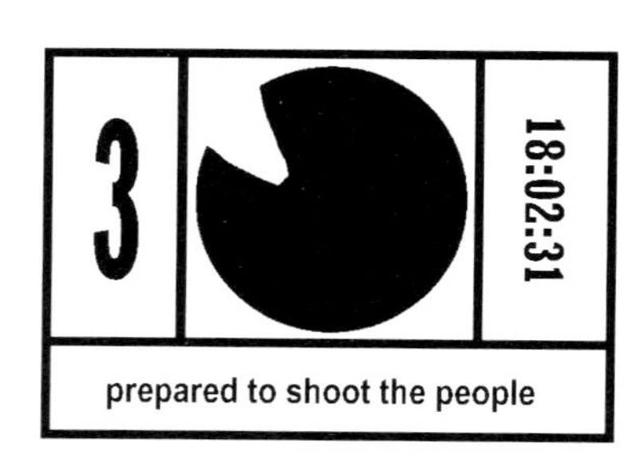

8:16am 11 April 2005

5.20am 12 April 2005

8.00am 13 April 2005

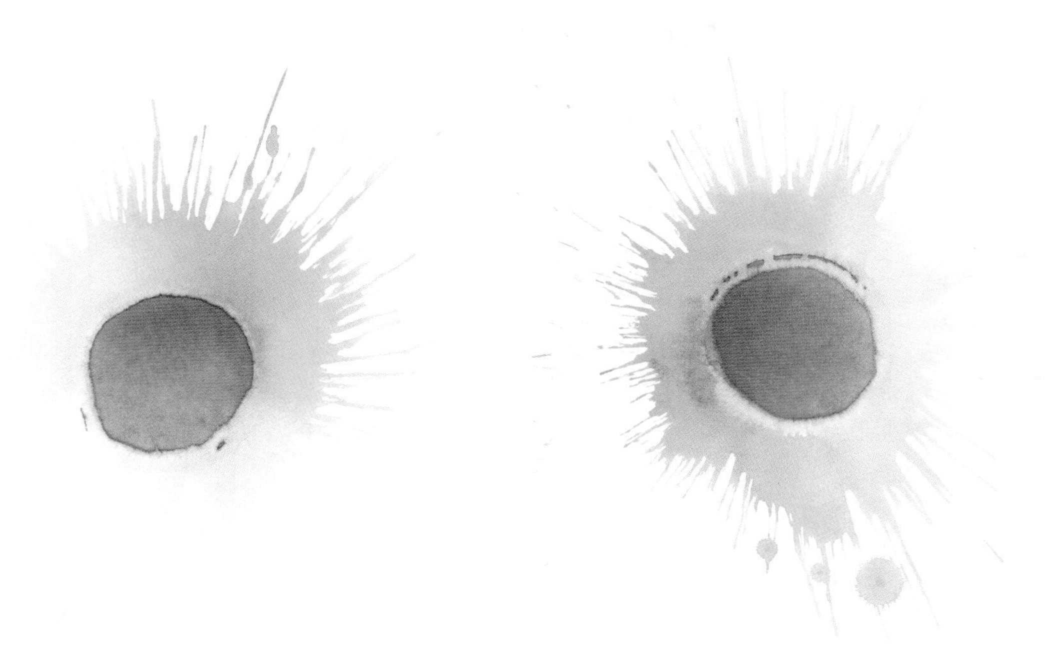

5.21am 14 April 2005

8.36am 15 April 2005

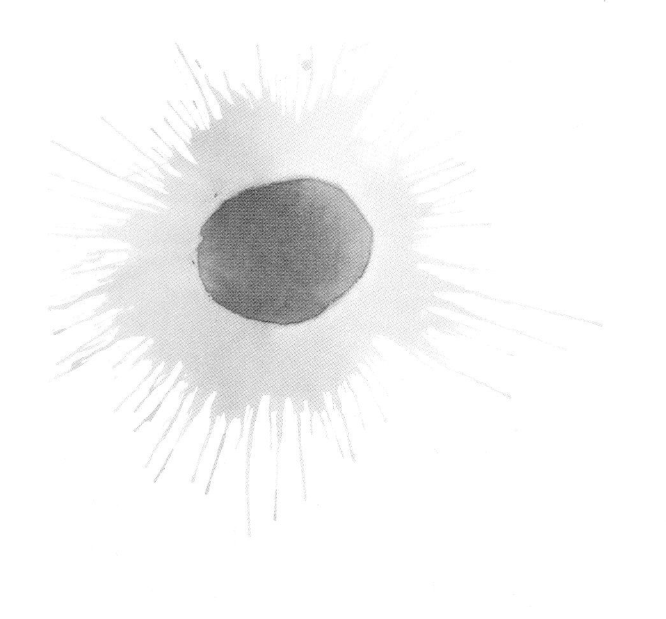

8:17 am 20 April 2005

Tony Kemplen

Born: 1959
Nationality: British
Lives: Sheffield
Title: *Eating pizza while watching the news*
Location: Page-based commission for this publication
Website: www.kemplen.co.uk

Old habits die hard, and one of mine over the last 15 years has been eating pizza while watching the evening news on the TV. There have been various artistic by-products from this activity, including a series of *Leaning towers of pizza* collages and an artist's book *Margherita margereater*, the latter leading a reviewer in Art Monthly to comment that, if nothing else, someone should save me from my diet (rather unfairly in my view, as I only do it twice a week, and augment the basic pizza with carefully chosen nutritious extras).

On Tuesday 8 March 2005, a normal day, which also happened to be my mother's 75th birthday, I set up a video camera to record the progress on my plate, and arranged the video recorder to tape the news. This raw data was painstakingly transcribed and annotated to come up with a series of sound bites and still frames to document the precise moment when each portion entered my mouth.

Each bite of the pizza was accompanied by a nugget of news; tomatoes with an alleged IRA murder, mushrooms meet Michael Jackson, sweet corn and the seed corn of Chinese democracy, olives and killer blood clots, chillies with the fiery special effects of the long awaited new series of Dr Who, and extra cheese for Charles and Camilla.

Georges Perec, the habitual chronicler of the mundane, died a few days short of his 46th birthday. In his publication *Attempt at an Inventory of the Liquid and Solid Foodstuffs Ingurgitated by Me in the Course of the Year Nineteen Hundred and Seventy-Four*, he admits to having eaten only one pizza. Writing this a few days before my own 46th birthday, I am comforted by the thought that if Perec's death was related to the paucity of pizza in his diet, my 100 per year habit might not be such a bad thing after all.

IRA
25,000
deaths
1
2
3
4
5
6
7
8
9
10
11
12
13
14
15
16
17
18
19
20
21
22
23
24
25
26
27
28
29

8 MAR 2005

Day-to-Day Data is supported by:

Danielle Arnaud
contemporary art

Support for individual artists' projects:

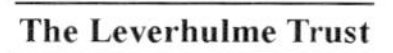

Ben Highmore is Senior Lecturer in cultural studies at the University of the West of England, Bristol. He is the author of *Everyday Life and Cultural Theory* and editor of *The Everyday Life Reader* (both published by Routledge, 2002). His latest book is called *Cityscapes: Cultural Readings in the Material and Symbolic City* and is published by Palgrave Macmillan (2005). A book on the historian and cultural theorist Michel de Certeau is scheduled to appear in 2006.

Kris Cohen is a research fellow in the Department of Sociology at the University of Surrey. For the past two years he has worked in the INCITE research group (www.soc.surrey.ac.uk/incite) and is currently funded by the Economic and Social Research Council (ESRC) to study the uses of personal photography online. He is also a member of low-fi, an artist collective which runs the net art locator (www.low-fi.org.uk) and which curates and commissions networked art projects.

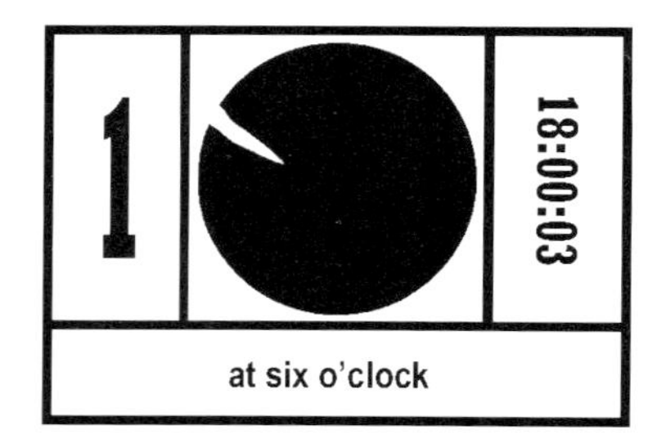

Abigail Reynolds' *Dictionary Ranges: Diagram of 'table'* is a result of a period of residency, supported by the Leverhulme Trust, at the Oxford English Dictionary (OED). Abigail Reynolds would like to thank the Oxford University Press and particularly the Director and Chief Etymologist at the OED.

Jem Finer's *On Earth as in Heaven* is a result of a period of residency, supported by the Calouste Gulbenkian Foundation, at the Astrophysics Department of Oxford University.

Lucy Kimbell's *Untitled (Physical Bar Charts)* is a result of a Creative and Performing Arts Fellowship, supported by the Arts and Humanities Research Council, at the Ruskin School of Drawing and Fine Art.

Angel Row Gallery would like to thank Ellie Harrison for curating the exhibition, publication and website and the artists for their participation. We would also like to thank the collaborating organisations and in particular, Danielle Arnaud; Jo Bushnell and Susie Clark at Aspex Gallery; and Helen Sloan at SCAN.

Ellie Harrison would like to thank for their help and support with the project: Jon Burgerman, Bernard Harrison, Anne Harrison and Flo Harrison; Steven Barrett for his help getting the project started; Angel Row Gallery staff, Aspex Gallery staff and Danielle Arnaud; Clarissa Corfe and Alison Lloyd from Arts Council England; Sarah Cook, Saul Albert and Isis Arts for their help with the initial selection process; all of the artists, Ben Highmore and Kris Cohen for their enthusiasm and fantastic contributions; Fraser Muggeridge and Sarah Newitt for their patience, skill and commitment in designing and compiling this publication.

Day-to-Day Data exhibition dates:

Angel Row Gallery, Nottingham:
20 July – 7 September 2005

Aspex Gallery, Portsmouth:
17 September – 29 October 2005

Danielle Arnaud contemporary art, London:
10 March – 23 April 2006

www.daytodaydata.com

First published in 2005 on the occasion
of the exhibition *Day-to-Day Data* by
Angel Row Gallery, Central Library Building,
3 Angel Row, Nottingham, NG1 6HP
T: + 44 (0) 115 915 2869
E: angelrow.info@nottinghamcity.gov.uk
www.angelrowgallery.com

All rights reserved. No part of this book may
be reproduced, stored in a retrieval system, or
transmitted, in any form by any means, electronic,
mechanical, photocopying, recording or otherwise
without the prior written permission of the
publisher.

© 2005 Angel Row Gallery, Ellie Harrison,
Ben Highmore, Kris Cohen, the artists and
photographers.

British Library Cataloguing in Publication Data.
A British Library CIP record is available.

ISBN 0 905634 71 3
Edited by Ellie Harrison, Jim Waters and Helen Jones
Proof-read by Bernard Harrison and Anne Harrison
Designed by Fraser Muggeridge studio
Printed in Belgium by Die Keure

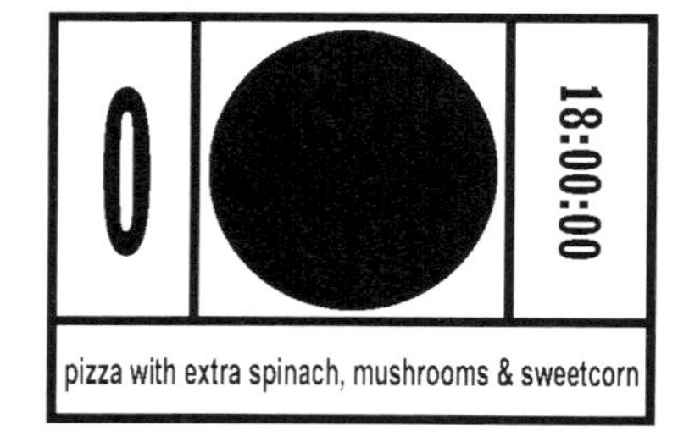
0
18:00:00
pizza with extra spinach, mushrooms & sweetcorn